THE OFFICIAL ITV SPORT Champions League Guide

CW01584119

AUTHOR'S NOTE:
In a number of instances domestic records are not available.
This is usually where available records clash with those released by UEFA.

Special thanks for assistance with text and research to Kevin Connolly and also to Andrew Warshaw.

This is a Carlton Book

Copyright © 1999 Carlton Books Ltd

First published in 1999 by Carlton Books

10 9 8 7 6 5 4 3 2 1

First edition 1999

All rights reserved. No part of this publication may be reproduced, stored in a retrieval system, or transmitted, in any form or by any means without the prior written permission of the publisher, nor be otherwise circulated in any form of binding or cover other than that in which it is published and without a similar condition being imposed on the subsequent purchaser.

A CIP catalogue record for this book is available from the British Library

ISBN 1 85868 828 0

Project Editor: Chris Hawkes
Project Art Direction: Brian Flynn
Picture Research: Catherine Costelloe
Production: Bob Bhamra

Printed and bound in Great Britain by
Butler & Tanner Ltd, Frome and London

Carlton Books Limited
20 Mortimer Street
London W1N 7RD

THE OFFICIAL ITV SPORT

Champions League Guide

THE COMPLETE GUIDE TO EUROPE'S PREMIER CLUB EVENT

KIER RADNEDGE

CARLTON BOOKS

Contents

AMSTEL
Canon
MasterCard
PlayStation
nutella
AMSTEL BEER
Canon

(Above) Poised to bring TV viewers all the action. (Previous spread) The stage is set for another glory night.

Media Focus

Just as the Champions League has entered a new era, viewers throughout the United Kingdom will be able to see the action of the world's premier club event as it unfolds, blow by blow, like they have never seen it before.

ITV's coverage is bigger and better than ever. Last year we brought live coverage of 11 matches throughout the tournament, from the preliminary stages right through to that glorious night in Barcelona where Manchester United kept us all on the edge of our seats until securing that famous, last-gasp victory and helping themselves to a historic treble.

This year, in keeping with the increasing stature of the tournament, ITV is screening 17 live matches from the group stages right through to the final.

With a late night highlights programme covering the complete Champions League scene to follow, Wednesday night truly is European football night for terrestrial viewers. And on Tuesday nights, there's a brand-new, peak-time highlights show on ITV – making a total of 49 Champions League programmes on terrestrial television. For those of you with ONdigital, there is an added opportunity to follow the progress of the British clubs with live matches on Tuesday, plus an alternative live game on ITV2 on Wednesdays.

ITV is making the best football more accessible than ever. Britain's best-loved football presenter, Desmond Lynam, heads an impressive ITV line-up featuring England's coach, Kevin Keegan, former England managers, Terry Venables and Glenn Hoddle, as well as former internationals, Ally McCoist and Barry Venison. Bob Wilson and Gabby Yorath present the two highlight shows, and in the commentary box Clive Tyldesley and Peter Drury call the shots, with expert comment from the likes of Ron Atkinson and David Pleat.

ITV is committed to bring you all the drama of this prestigious competition. All you have to do is sit back and enjoy what promises to be the greatest European season ever.

Galatasaray fans welcome the opposition to "Hell" with typical enthusiasm.

1 Introduction

EUROPEAN football has seen nothing quite like the 1999–2000 UEFA Champions League. It is more than the old European Cup revamped. It is the foundation for a futuristic format to suit the new millennium – and help to maintain soccer's ascendancy over all the other sports clamouring for public attention.

Appropriately, considering the development of association football, even the European club revolution began with the English. That was back in the early 1950s when Wolverhampton Wanderers scored two famous victories in club friendlies over Honved, who boasted the nucleus of the great Hungarian national team of the time, and Moscow Spartak.

English newspapers instantly proclaimed Wolves the champions of Europe.

That infuriated Gabriel Hanot, former French international turned editor of the Paris sports newspaper *L'Equipe*. He had seen what was developing around Alfredo Di Stefano at Real Madrid, he had seen the thrilling power of a Milan team inspired by their Swedish Gre-No-Li trio (Gren, Nordahl, Liedholm) and he was thrilled by the potential of a "local" Reims club with a twinkle-toed creative centre-forward named Raymond Kopa.

> *"This way we can give more to the top associations and open the door wider to the smaller associations. We have found a good balance between sporting, political and commercial considerations. The new format is easy to understand. We start with eight groups of four, go to four groups of four and switch then to a classical cup system. It's a big step forward to ensure a prosperous future for European football ... under the guidance of UEFA."*
>
> *UEFA president Lennart Johansson*

Hanot took out a page of his newspaper to propose a "real" European club cup. He invited representatives of leading clubs from all over Europe to a meeting in Paris, and they laid down the concept of a midweek knock-out competition based on the two-leg aggregate system. Thus was born the European Champion Clubs' Cup with a knock-out format whose simplicity and quality set the standard for international competition in South America, Africa, Asia, Oceania and in Central and North America ... everywhere around the world where football is played and where international rivalries can be played out between two goal frames around

UEFA President, Lennart Johannson, has helped to forge European football's greatest event.

100 metres apart.

The sense of football history will be shared by Iceland's Steingrimur Johannesson – because he was the man who fired IBV's only goal against SK Tirana of Albania all the way back on July 13, 1999, when the curtain went up on the new Champions Cup in front of a mere 790 fans.

That first qualifying round produced no surprises, but there were plenty of goals. Moldova's Zimbru Chisinau (against St Patrick's Athletic), Skonto Riga of Latvia (against Jeunesse d'Esch of Luxembourg) and Yugoslavia's Partizan Belgrade (against Flora of Estonia) all hit 10 goals over the two legs.

There was no such high scoring in the second qualifying round, though Molde, notably, hit back from 2–0 down after the first leg to beat CSKA Moscow 4–0 (4–2 on aggregate) and Maribor of Slovenia were very nearly upset by Belgium's Genk despite winning the first leg 5–1 at home. The only two clubs with European success behind them – ex-Cup-winners' Cup holders Kiev Dynamo and Rangers – both cruised through at the expense of Zhalgiris of Lithuania and Haka of Finland.

Rangers also sprang the surprise of the third qualifying round when they beat the UEFA Cup holders, Parma, while other unexpected casualties were Spain's Mallorca, who had been runners-up in the last Cup-winners' Cup Final to Lazio. The other disappointed third-round failures were French club Lyon who had spent heavily during the summer, including a domestic-record £10 million on Brazilian striker, Sonny Anderson, from Barcelona. Against all the odds, they then found the Slovenes of Maribor Teatanic too tenacious and lost both 1–0 at home and 2–0 away.

So, with the television cash rolling in and the star-decorated football logo unifying Europe's top stadia, everything was set for the stars of the glittering new Champions League show to take the stage.

Not that the evolutionary process throughout the 1990s had been an easy one. UEFA began the redevelopment work in 1991–92. After 36 years of loyalty to the simple, home-and-away, two-leg knock-out system, UEFA experimented by organising the eight quarter-finalists into two groups of four teams, playing each other home and away. The winners of the groups went directly to the Final.

The following season, 1992–93, the experiment was formalised as the Champions League. A further refinement in 1993–94 saw single-leg, knock-out semi-finals reintroduced – a development which answered complaints about the number of "dead" matches when the group winners had already been decided.

Season 1994–95 saw major change. The group stage was expanded to four groups of four clubs and played out in the autumn sector of the season. The knock-out quarter-finals were restored and the semi-finals reverted to two legs apiece.

Just when fans around Europe had grown comfortable with this pattern, so it was altered again. Western European television channels, dissatisfied that their huge cash investment did not guarantee the reward of one of their own clubs at the heart of the action, helped persuade UEFA to expand yet again. Thus, in 1997–98 the group stage was expanded to six groups of four clubs – and, in 1998–99, the runners-up from Europe's top leagues were also welcomed to the dizzy heights of the Champions League.

Even those developments were not enough to satisfy the big clubs whose budgets were stretched up to and beyond the limits by players whose wage demands had soared sky high in the wake of the Bosman ruling of December 1995.

No longer were players tied to their clubs by a transfer fee when their contracts expired. On the other hand, no longer were the clubs bound by anachronistic restrictions on how many – or, rather, how few – foreign players they could line up.

The undercurrent of dissatisfaction with the money on offer through the Champions League fuelled proposals for a breakaway European Super League. The putative project was co-ordinated by a Milan-based promotional company, Media Partners.

Chelsea captain, Dennis Wise, powers past Riga's Alexander Rekhviashvili during the qualifying round.

Eventually UEFA came up with proposals of its own which – temporarily at least – defused the breakaway time bomb. The European federation gambled successfully that the likes of Real Madrid, Manchester United, Arsenal and Juventus would opt for less money, but greater security, within the UEFA family rather than out of it in the Super League cold.

UEFA's brave new Champions League world for the season which ushers in the new millennium had thus been constructed around a central phase featuring 32 clubs split into eight groups of four. But around 70 clubs had initial right of entry at various qualifying stages. For example, Italy, Germany and Spain, the top three countries in the UEFA ranking list, each had four places – two in the groups and two in the third qualifying round.

How long the big clubs remain satisfied depends on the financial fall-out. UEFA offered £340 million to be shared among clubs and associations while the winning club's share would rise to more than £15 million – before adding in gate receipts, etc.

Clearly, the chance of remaining within the establishment comfort zone helped mollify leading UEFA-sceptics, such as Real Madrid president, Lorenzo Sanz, and

Rangers' Michael Mols in action during his side's impressive victory over Parma.

Bayern Munich general manager, Uli Hoeness.

One consequence of the launch of the new Champions League was the death of the Cup-winners' Cup after almost 40 years. The new UEFA Cup swallowed up the Cup-winners' Cup thus guaranteeing top countries up to five places in the secondary European tournament.

Access to the new Champions League – the title remains – must depend on a country's status in the 51-nation UEFA rankings. The champions of roughly half UEFA's membership entered the first knock-out qualifying round in July. The runners-up of the six countries ranked 10 to 15, plus the champions of countries 16 to 26 (including Scotland), entered the second qualifying round in late July/early August.

The winners of those knock-out rounds then proceeded to the third qualifying round where they were joined by the third and fourth-placed clubs of Italy, Germany and Spain, the third-placed clubs of France, Holland and England plus a further assortment of champions and runners-up.

Finally, on September 13, the formal Champions League itself began with matches played on both Tuesdays and Wednesdays to maximise possible television income.

Of course there are drawbacks – one being the increased pressure within an already crowded fixtures programme. The eventual winners of the Champions League will have played a minimum of 17 games and even more if they came through the qualifying stages. That was one consideration which prompted Manchester United's controversial withdrawal from the FA Cup to play in the new World Club Championship in Brazil in January 2000.

Also, in the strictest terms, this is no longer exclusively a Champions League. But UEFA president Lennart Johansson justified the title, after some liguistic contortions by saying: "The Champions Cup has now become the league to find the champions of Europe – hence the Champions League."

The entire competition will have lasted less than 10 months by the time the final, on May 24, is over and the winners and losers have cried – with respective happiness and disappointment – over their medals.

Champions, Manchester United, confidently expected to survive an opening group which included Sturm Graz of Austria and Marseille plus an old rival in Argentine Osvaldo Ardiles, once of Tottenham and now coach of Croatia Zagreb.

However Arsenal, the English club in Group B, appeared to face a tougher task after being drawn with Fiorentina, AIK Stockholm and a Barcelona side who had invested heavily in Dutch talent in their bid to become European champions for the first time since 1992.

Not that Barcelona's Spanish rivals, Real Madrid, were spectators. The record seven-times holders had also splashed out on the likes of Nicolas Anelka, Steve McManaman and Elvir Baljic with the ambition of regaining their crown. They did not expect any problems disposing of first-round rivals such as FC Porto, Olympiakos Piraeus and rank outsiders, Molde – who found themselves in the Champions League proper despite never having won the championship of Norway.

One other club with their eyes focused on final glory were Lazio, last winners of the Cup-winners' Cup. They lost their leadership of the Italian league on the last day of last season – despite having led for much of the way.

The world-record, £31-million, summer sale of centre forward Christian Vieri to Inter shocked Lazio fans, but owner Sergio Cragnotti immediately invested the cash in a string of squad-strengthening stars. They included Argentine playmaker, Juan Veron, from Parma and up-and-coming Italian striker, Simone Inzaghi, from Piacenza.

Lazio also entered the Champions League proud in the knowledge that they had succeeded where the rest of Europe had failed last season – in defeating Manchester United for the European Supercup in Monaco at the end of August.

Whether any one else would follow suit in the Champions League itself is, of course, another matter.

2 The Teams

A competition which began way back in July, which passed through three preliminary stages, started for proper with eight groups of four teams. What follows is a run-down of the 32 remaining teams who have the right to fight for the title of "Champions of Europe".

For Milan's Oliver Bierhoff, winning the national league provides a chance to perform on the greatest stage.

Formed 1904 **Coach** Christoph Daum **Stadium** Bayarena
Capacity 25,050 **Address** Postfach 120140, 51349 Leverkusen
Website: www.bayer04.de

Bayer Leverkusen

THE rise of Bayer Leverkusen has been one of the great success stories of modern German football. It also proves that big-city clubs do not have a monopoly on success.

Bayer do not have a German league title to their name and they have won the cup only once, in 1993, when they beat Hertha Berlin Amateurs 1–0 in the final. But they are one of that exclusive band of German clubs who can boast European success, having carried off the UEFA Cup in 1988.

That remains the peak of Bayer's achievement – and a memorable one since they lost the first leg of the final 3–0 to Espanol Barcelona yet fought back against the odds to win their own home leg by the same margin and then triumph in the subsequent penalty shoot-out. The decade since then has been spent establishing their presence as a permanent force in the Bundesliga – though coach Christoph Daum knows Bayer have a long way to go to catch up with Bayern Munich in terms of both wealth and allure. As Daum once said: "Bayern are above the rest – but we want to be the best of the rest."

Sensible management and shrewd work in the transfer market matches the image of the club reflected in its tidy,

Squad List

No.	Name	Date of birth	Position	Nationality	Domestic apps/goals	European Cup apps/goals
1	**Adam MATYSEK**	19.07.1968	Goalkeeper	Poland	37 / 0	4 / 0
20	**Frank JURIC**	28.10.1973	Goalkeeper	Austria/Croatia	0 / 0	0 / 0
23	**Dirk HEINEN**	03.12.1970	Goalkeeper	Germany	107 / 0	13 / 0
2	**Robert KOVAC**	06.04.1974	Defender	Croatia/Germany	73 / 0	9 / 0
3	**Markus HAPPE**	11.02.1972	Defender	Germany	185 / 8	26 / 1
5	**Jens NOWOTNY**	11.01.1974	Defender	Germany	195 / 8	14 / 0
6	**Boris ZIVKOVIC**	15.11.1975	Defender	Croatia	39 / 3	8 / 0
14	**Torben HOFFMANN**	27.10.1974	Defender	Germany	21 / 2	0 / 0
21	**Zoran MAMIC**	30.09.1971	Defender	Croatia	54 / 4	7 / 1
4	**Jorg REEB**	06.01.1972	Midfielder	Germany	90 / 6	2 / 0
7	**ROBSON Ponte**	06.11.1976	Midfielder	Brazil	4 / 1	0 / 0
8	**ZE ROBERTO**	06.07.1974	Midfielder	Brazil	35 / 4	0 / 0
10	**EMERSON Ferreira da Rosa**	04.04.1976	Midfielder	Brazil	56 / 6	12 / 4
13	**Michael BALLACK**	26.09.1976	Midfielder	Germany	47 / 4	6 / 0
18	**Frankie HEJDUK**	05.08.1974	Midfielder	USA	13 / 1	0 / 0
19	**Vratislav GRESKO**	24.07.1977	Midfielder	Slovakia	1 / 0	4 / 0
22	**Stefan BEINLICH**	13.01.1972	Midfielder	Germany	120 / 33	12 / 5
24	**Daryoush YAZDANI**	02.06.1977	Midfielder	Iran	0 / 0	0 / 0
25	**Bernd SCHNEIDER**	17.11.1973	Midfielder	Germany	37 / 4	0 / 0
28	**Carsten RAMELOW**	20.03.1974	Midfielder	Germany	111 / 10	13 / 0
9	**Ulf KIRSTEN**	04.12.1965	Forward	Germany	262 / 143	51 / 29
11	**Thomas REICHENBERGER**	14.10.1974	Forward	Germany	21 / 4	2 / 1
12	**Thomas BRDARIC**	23.01.1975	Forward	Germany	22 / 2	0 / 0
16	**Miroslav SPIZAK**	13.01.1979	Forward	Poland	0 / 0	0 / 0
27	**Oliver NEUVILLE**	01.05.1973	Forward	Germany	54 / 24	13 / 1

purpose-built Ulrich Haberland stadium, which features both a fast-food restaurant and a hotel. Bayer have also been among the leaders in German football in projecting their own brand image with television adverts urging viewers to get the "Bayer 04 feeling".

Nor do Leverkusen's players and coaching staff concede anything to Bayern out on the pitch. In 1996–97, Bayer gave Munich a tough ride of it before finishing as league runners-up, the following term they ended third – one place behind Bayern – and last season they were again runners-up to their Bavarian rivals. Any one who dares to suggest that Bayer will always be second-best is given short shrift.

"Of course it is possible for us to overtake them," says Brazil midfielder Emerson Ferreira. "We all want it badly and I really believe we can make it." It would be hugely ironic if Bayer could make the point by outstripping Bayern in the Champions League this season.

Leverkusen will rely on the creative skills in midfield of Emerson and Ze Roberto, their two Brazilians. Ze Roberto cost a club record fee of £8 million from Flamengo of Rio de Janeiro. He struggled to adjust initially to both the football and lifestyle in Germany, but soon became a favourite with fans.

"I just needed time to show what I am capable of," he says. "I can still improve."

The danger man in attack is international veteran Ulf Kirsten, one of the last heroes of football in the former East Germany. Kirsten, who played 49 times for the GDR and has since added 14 goals in more than 30 international appearances for the unified Germany, has twice been the Bundesliga's top scorer.

Ze Roberto: a club-record fee and midfield inspiration.

Leverkusen's defensive security rests on skipper Jens Nowotny who is, for many critics, the best libero or sweeper in the Bundesliga – ahead of the ageing Lothar Matthaus of Bayern Munich and otherwise without a challenger since injuries sidelined Borussia Dortmund's Matthias Sammer.

It is no surprise that Nowotny has grown impatient for international recognition. Starring in the Champions League should do his cause no harm.

"For three years I've been hearing that my time will come. I have to become the national team's libero some day. But when?" says Nowotny.

Taller and more powerful than Matthaus, Nowotny is certainly better in the air and he posesses a delicacy of touch which enables him to move the ball forward with speed and accuracy on the counter-attack. Whether Daum instructs Bayer tactically in 3-5-2 or 4-3-3 makes no difference to the versatile Nowotny.

Daum's major concern is the fixture pressure induced by the expansion of the Champions League. He says: "It's terrific to be rubbing shoulders with all these big clubs, but the expansion means there are more games than ever this season and we do run a risk of burn-out. That's why we have tried to give our squad greater strength in depth.

"One thing about the new Champions League is certain, however. With so many teams and so many games, the club who wins will certainly deserve it."

Bayer Leverkusen Records

European honours: UEFA Cup 1987–88

Record European victory: 6–1 v Dynamo Tbilisi, Champions League qualifying round 1997–98

Record European defeat: 0–4 v Monaco, Champions League group phase 1997–98

Club records: Rüdiger Vollborn (401 Bundesliga matches), Ulf Kirsten (142 Bundesliga goals)

Record scorer in Europe: Ulf Kirsten, 21

Record attendance: 27,600 (v Köln, May 8th, 1993)

Formed 1927 **Coach** Valerii Lobanovski **Stadium** Olypiyskyi **Capacity** 82,300 **Address** vul. Hrushevskoho 3, 252 001 Kyiv

Dynamo Kiev

DYNAMO Kiev's surge to the semi-finals of the UEFA Champions League last season thrilled Ukrainian fans who love nothing better than seeing their own football go from strength to strength compared with neighbouring Russia.

Olexander Shovkovskyi: Ukraine's No. 1 through the Euro 2000 qualifiers.

Kiev's success has revived memories of the years when the club dominated Soviet soccer and twice won the European Cup-winners' Cup, but they still resented the manner in which their achievements were used by Moscow for USSR sporting propaganda.

The bitterness continued even after Ukraine split away from the fragmenting Soviet Union in the early 1990s. The Russian federation not only grabbed the one available qualifing place in the 1994 World Cup – meaning Ukraine had to wait a further four years for a place at the top table – but many of Kiev's best players such as Viktor Onopko, Ilya Tsymbalar, Sergei Yuran and Oleg Salenko were pressured into declaring a football allegiance to Russia rather than their homeland.

Now, however, the tables are being turned.

Kiev have dominated Ukraine domestic football since independence. That was no surprise. But the fact that the club has been able to make a meaningful impression at international level owes much to the return to command of Valeri Lobanovski, their veteran coach.

Lobanovsky, boss of Kiev when they won the Cup-winners' Cup in 1975 and 1986, returned to the club for a third stint late in 1997. "The coach for all times and all nations," was how he was described during a state reception for the officials and players – an ironic reference back to a label once claimed by the Soviet dictator, Josef Stalin.

Lobanovski is a master of the disciplined scientific approach to physical preparation of his players and is a past master of the tactical formulae designed both to bring the best out of his own players and shut down the attacking avenues of opponents. His legendary achievements have also made him an inspiring tutor to even modern Ukraine's new young talents.

President Grigory Surkis has no doubt about the club's potential. He says: "We dream of victory in the Champions League. It really is within

Squad List

No.	Name	Date of birth	Position	Nationality	Domestic apps/goals	European Cup apps/goals
1	**Olexander SHOVKOVSKYI**	02.01.1975	Goalkeeper	Ukraine	– / –	42 / 0
12	**Viacheslav KERNOZENKO**	04.06.1976	Goalkeeper	Ukraine	– / –	1 / 0
13	**Vsevolod ROMANENKO**	24.03.1977	Goalkeeper	Ukraine	– / –	0 / 0
4	**Olexander HOLOVKO**	06.01.1972	Defender	Ukraine	– / –	37 / 2
5	**Vladyslav VASCHUK**	02.01.1975	Defender	Ukraine	– / –	35 / 2
6	**Yurii DMYTRULIN**	10.02.1975	Defender	Ukraine	– / –	28 / 0
7	**Kakha KALADZE**	27.02.1978	Defender	Georgia	– / –	28 / 1
17	**Serhii FEDOROV**	18.02.1975	Defender	Ukraine	– / –	3 / 0
21	**Volodymyr YEZERSKIY**	15.11.1976	Defender	Ukraine	– / –	0 / 0
23	**Olexander RADCHENKO**	19.07.1976	Defender	Ukraine	– / –	7 / 0
26	**Andrii NESMACHNYI**	28.02.1979	Defender	Ukraine	- / -	- / -
2	**Alexandre KHATSKEVICH**	19.10.1973	Midfielder	Belarus	– / –	30 / 2
3	**Alexei GUERASSIMENKO**	17.12.1970	Midfielder	Russia	– / –	12 / 1
9	**Vitalii KOSSOVSKYI**	11.08.1973	Midfielder	Poland/Ukraine	– / –	35 / 2
14	**Andrii HUSIN**	1.12.1972	Midfielder	Ukraine	– / –	28 / 3
15	**Artem IACHKIN**	29.04.1975	Midfielder	Russia	– / –	4 / 0
18	**Vassyl KARDASH**	14.01.1973	Midfielder	Ukraine	– / –	21 / 1
19	**Serguei KORMILTSEV**	22.01.1974	Midfielder	Russia	– / –	4 / 0
20	**Dmytro MYKHAILENKO**	13.07.1973	Midfielder	Ukraine	– / –	27 / 1
8	**Valiantsin BIALKEVICH**	27.01.1973	Forward	Belarus	– / –	24 / 5
10	**Oleh VENHLINSKYI**	21.03.1978	Forward	Ukraine	– / –	3 / 1
11	**Serhii REBROV**	03.06.1974	Forward	Russia/Ukraine	– / –	47 / 20
16	**Maksim SHATSKIKH**	30.08.1978	Forward	Uzbekistan	– / –	4 / 4
22	**Serhii KONOVALOV**	01.03.1972	Forward	Ukraine	– / –	9 / 0
24	**Olexander KOSSYRIN**	18.06.1977	Forward	Ukraine	– / –	0 / 0

our power to bring the Cup to Kiev."

But the club's European progress has not been without its pitfalls. Kiev were expelled from the Champions League in 1995, after only one match, for allegedly trying to bribe the Spanish referee, Antonio Lopez Nieto, with expensive fur coats. The club were banned for a further three years, but UEFA later decided, on appeal, to commute the sentence as a gesture of compassion towards a Ukraine game which is in desperate need of the kudos and cash which the Champions League brings.

Kiev thus returned to the battleground and the attacking finesse of Andryi Shevchenko and Serhii Rebrov took them past Lens, Arsenal, Panathinaikos and Real Madrid before they were edged out in the semi-finals, 4–3 on aggregate by Bayern Munich.

The price for success was an irristible £12 million offer from Milan for star striker Shevchenko. But Kiev have put the money to good use in strengthening their squad for the present campaign.

Goalkeeper Olexander Shovkovskyi remains his country's first choice in the European Championship, while the sweeping talents of skipper Olexander Holovko means that Kiev have barely felt the departure of long-serving Oleh Luzhnyi to Arsenal. Lobanovski has renewed his midfield with the arrivals of Serhii Kormiltsev and Kakha Kaladze, while up front, Rebrov has had to build a new striking partnership with the Uzbek forward, Maksim Shatskih.

Kiev's success is vital to the entire economy of the Ukraine game. They still play against a troubled social background, however, as Ukraine struggles to build an independent economy and find its own political place in the new, post-cold war Europe.

At least in Dynamo Kiev, the country could hardly boast a better standard-bearer across the continent.

Dynamo Kiev Records

European honours: Cup-winners' Cup 1974–75, 1985–86

Record European victory: 8–0 v Barry Town, Champions League preliminary round 1998–99

Record European defeat: 0–5 v Benfica, Champions League group phase 1991–92

Club records: Oleg Blokhin (432 matches and 211 goals)

Record scorer in Europe: Oleg Blokhin, 23

Record attendance: 100,164 (v Celtic FC, October 4th, 1967)

Formed 1900 **Coach** Sven-Goran Eriksson **Stadium** Stadio Olimpico **Capacity** 82,922 **Address** Via Umberto Novaro 32, 00195 Roma **Website** www.sslazio.it

Lazio

WHAT can Lazio achieve without Christian Vieri? That's the question which the Roman club must answer, as they prepare for their first assault on the Champions League.

The last – and only time – they won Serie A, in 1974, Lazio were banned from European competition because of serious misbehaviour after a Fairs Cup tie against Arsenal. Now they are in the big one for real and expectations are huge.

Marcelo Salas: much will depend on the Chilean striker.

Before last season's Cup-winners' Cup final victory over Mallorca, coach Sven-Goran Eriksson said: "This is the strongest squad I've ever worked with. Stronger even than the Roma side which reached the 1984 European Cup final. [They lost to Liverpool on penalties.]

"That Roma team included great talents like Falcao, Toninho Cerezo and Giuseppe Giannini, but they didn't have the depth Lazio have now." That was before Vieri left

Vieri, the £31-million man, marked his Inter debut with a hat-trick as his new club began the Serie A season with a 3–0 demolition of Verona. "Now you can see why we paid so much for him," said Inter coach Marcello Lippi.

Lazio's efforts to sign an immediate replacement foundered on the rocks that are Nicolas Anelka and his brothers. Arsenal's centre forward chose Real Madrid instead.

But Sven-Goran Eriksson's team have recruited other new forwards – one for the future, one as a stopgap for the present. Simone Inzaghi, younger brother of Juventus striker Pippo, arrived from Piacenza, for £10.5 million. He scored 15 Serie A goals for Piacenza last season. Anywhere near that figure for Lazio would bring a beaming smile to Eriksson's face.

Inzaghi represents Lazio's future. By contrast, Kennet Andersson, the giant Swede signed from Bologna, is a short-term buy. His aerial presence gives Lazio options beyond a cultured build-up.

Lazio already have quality strikers, in the Chilean Marcelo Salas and the Croat Alen Boksic. Much will depend on ex-River Plate star Salas, so prolific last season. But neither has the physical presence of Vieri, the Australian-Italian who is able to slug it out with the toughest defenders.

Roberto Mancini, now 34, can still play up front – though Eriksson is more likely to use him in a withdrawn midfield role, or as a deluxe substitute.

Lazio have certainly strengthened that midfield. The Argentinian international Diego Simeone came from Inter as part of the Vieri deal

Lazio also paid £18.5 million to Parma for Argentina's midfield inspiration Juan Veron – who imposed himself in pre-season friendlies and looked a class act. Veron's scoring record has been nothing special, but judging by early evidence, Eriksson believes Veron has the potential to chip in with important goals.

Matias Almeyda, signed from Seville in 1997, is another

Lazio Records

European honours: Cup-winners' Cup 1998–99

Record European victory: 5–0 v Boavista, UEFA Cup 1st round 1977–78; 5–0 v Omonia Nicosia, UEFA Cup 1st round 1995–96

Record European defeat: 0–6 v RC Lens, UEFA Cup 2nd round 1977–78

Club records: Aldo Puccinelli (339 matches in Serie A), Silvio Piola (143 goals in Serie A)

Record scorer in Europe: Giorgio Chinaglia, 11

Record attendance: 82,000 (v Vicenza Calcio 1986–87)

Argentinian with an important job. He is the ball winner, a defensive midfield player with a ferocious work rate.

Eriksson is a firm believer in the value of wide players. The Portuguese international, Sergio Conceicao, looks booked for the right side slot, with the Czech Pavel Nedved – scorer of so many valuable goals – on the left. Simeone and the Yugoslav Dejan Stankovic can play wide too, if needed.

Lazio's new-look side beat Manchester United in the European Super Cup final, prompting Sir Alex Feguson to predict that they would win the Italian league. That result has been a huge morale-booster. "Apart from the trophy itself, it proved we can beat anyone in Europe today," said Eriksson.

Lazio president, multi-millionaire Sergio Cragnotti wants nothing less. That's why the club's cheque book has been ever-open this summer.

The Roman club have not looked only for attackers. They have kept last season's defence intact, and added to it. Another Argentinian, 32-year-old Nestor Sensini, has been summoned from Parma for £1 million, to cover at centre half or right back.

The troops in front of goalkeeper, Luca Marchegiani, virtually pick themselves. The Yugoslav, Sinisa Mihaljovic, is a reliable central defender – and Lazio's dead ball expert. Stopper Alessandro Nesta, a Lazio player since he was 16, is the heart of the back line. Full backs Paolo Negro and Giuseppe Favalli complete a solid back four.

Last season, Lazio played nine games to win that last-ever Cup-winners' Cup. This season, as Eriksson says: "To win the Champions League, you have to play 17 games, which is half a Serie A season.

"Basic ideas about automatic choices have to change. Apart from the goalkeeper, no player can be expected to ride out the physical and mental stress of 60-plus matches at this level. We'll have to plan carefully to make the best use of our resources."

Squad List

No.	Name	Date of birth	Position	Nationality	Domestic apps/goals	European Cup apps/goals
1	**Luca MARCHEGIANI**	22.02.1966	Goalkeeper	Italy	307 / 0	54 / 0
12	**Emanuele CONCETTI**	03.06.1978	Goalkeeper	Italy	0 / 0	0 / 0
22	**Marco BALLOTTA**	03.04.1964	Goalkeeper	Italy	108 / 0	11 / 0
2	**Paolo NEGRO**	16.04.1972	Defender	Italy	213 / 15	36 / 2
5	**Giuseppe FAVALLI**	08.01.1972	Defender	Italy	274 / 6	26 / 1
6	**Roberto Nestor SENSINI**	12.10.1966	Defender	Argentina	233 / 14	41 / 6
11	**Sinisa MIHAJLOVIC**	20.02.1969	Defender	Yugoslavia	195 / 21	41 / 8
13	**Alessandro NESTA**	19.03.1976	Defender	Italy	113 / 1	22 / 1
15	**Giuseppe PANCARO**	26.08.1971	Defender	Italy	154 / 6	18 / 1
24	**FERNANDO M. COUTO Silva**	02.08.1969	Defender	Portugal	61 / 6	49 / 4
7	**SERGIO Paulo da CONCEICAO**	5.11.1974	Midfielder	Portugal	34 / 5	16 / 1
14	**Diego Pablo SIMONE**	28.04.1970	Midfielder	Argentina	90 / 15	26 / 7
16	**Attilio LOMBARDO**	06.01.1966	Midfielder	Italy	252 / 37	52 / 11
17	**Guerino GOTTARDI**	18.12.1970	Midfielder	Italy	70 / 1	17 / 1
18	**Pavel NEDVED**	30.08.1972	Midfielder	Czech Republic	81 / 19	41 / 13
20	**Dejan STANKOVIC**	11.09.1978	Midfielder	Yugoslavia	29 / 4	18 / 9
23	**Juan Sebastian VERON**	09.03.1975	Midfielder	Argentina	88 / 8	13 / 0
25	**Matias Jesus ALMEYDA**	21.12.1973	Midfielder	Argentina	46 / 1	14 / 0
8	**Alen BOKSIC**	21.01.1970	Forward	Croatia	119 / 30	33 / 13
9	**Jose Marcelo SALAS Meliano**	24.12.1974	Forward	Chile	32 / 15	7 / 5
10	**Roberto MANCINI**	27.11.1964	Forward	Italy	522 / 156	55 / 14
19	**Kennet ANDERSSON**	06.10.1967	Forward	Sweden	121 / 38	16 / 0
21	**Simone INZAGHI**	05.04.1976	Forward	Italy	32 / 16	1 / 0

Formed 1960 **Coach** Bojan Prasnikar **Stadium** Ljudski
Capacity 7,380 **Address** Mladinska 29, 2000 Maribor
Website www.nkmaribor.com

Maribor

MARIBOR have put Slovene football on the international map by reaching the Champions League group stage – and especially by defeating Belgium's Genk and big-spending French club Lyon to do so.

They are also the youngest club in the event, having been founded only in 1960. Originally Maribor played mainly in the regional section of the championship of the former Yugoslavia, without ever breaking through the ranks of the big clubs. They won the Slovene regional championship five times, but that was as far as it went. At nationwide Yugoslav level there were no league titles, no cup victories. Only notoriety when, on one occasion, Maribor were punished with enforced relegation after a bribery scandal.

But that was another era. Maribor fans have had plenty to cheer since Slovenia took advantage of the fragmentation of Yugoslavia to claim independence from Belgrade.

The first championship was staged in 1991–92. Olimpija from the capital, Ljubljana, dominated the early years, but Maribor made history by becoming the first cup winners of independent Slovenia. They upset Olimpija's double dreams by defeating them 4–3 in a penalty shootout after a 0–0 draw.

Maribor won the cup again in 1993 and 1995 to establish a reputation as a team for the big occasion, a tradition which should serve them well in the UEFA Champions League.

Squad List

No.	Name	Date of birth	Position	Nationality	Domestic apps/goals	European Cup apps/goals
1	**Luka GRESAK**	18.04.1973	Goalkeeper	Slovenia	– / –	3 / 0
12	**Tomasz MURKO**	07.02.1979	Goalkeeper	Slovenia	– / –	4 / 0
22	**Marko SIMEUNOVIC**	06.12.1967	Goalkeeper	Slovenia	– / –	22 / 1
2	**Martin PREGELJ**	06.05.1977	Defender	Slovenia	– / –	3 / 0
4	**Maumer VUGDALIC**	25.08.1977	Defender	Slovenia	– / –	10 / 0
5	**Matjaz KEK**	09.09.1961	Defender	Slovenia	– / –	15 / 0
6	**Gregor LUK**	29.12.1979	Defender	Slovenia	– / –	0 / 0
15	**Suad FILEKOVIC**	16.09.1978	Defender	Slovenia	– / –	2 / 0
18	**Geri CIPI**	28.02.1976	Defender	Albania	– / –	5 / 0
21	**Marinko GALIC**	22.04.1970	Defender	Slovenia	– / –	22 / 3
24	**Peter DIVJAK**	28.03.1979	Defender	Slovenia	– / –	0 / 0
25	**Matej MILJATOVIC**	23.06.1979	Defender	Slovenia	– / –	0 / 0
26	**Marinko SARKEZI**	03.05.1972	Defender	Slovenia	– / –	16 / 0
7	**Simon SESLAR**	05.04.1974	Midfielder	Slovenia	– / –	4 / 0
8	**Gregor ZIDAN**	05.10.1965	Midfielder	Slovenia	– / –	29 / 2
10	**Amir KARIC**	05.10.1965	Midfielder	Slovenia	– / –	14 / 2
16	**Mehmet DRAGUSHA**	09.10.1977	Midfielder	Yugoslavia	- / -	- / -
17	**Bostjan ZNUDERL**	17.01.1979	Midfielder	Slovenia	– / –	0 / 0
19	**Stipe BALAJIC**	7.09.1968	Midfielder	Croatia	– / –	10 / 3
20	**Dejan DJURANOVIC**	05.05.1968	Midfielder	Slovenia	– / –	26 / 2
9	**Damir PEKIC**	15.01.1979	Forward	Slovenia	– / –	1 / 0
11	**Dalibor FILIPOVIC**	28.09.1974	Forward	Croatia	– / –	9 / 4
14	**Ante SIMUNDZA**	28.09.1971	Forward	Slovenia	– / –	19 / 7
23	**Kliton BOZGO**	05.12.1971	Forward	Albania/Slovenia	– / –	23 / 11

Maribor have also developed a consistency which has been reflected in their recent domination of the championship – they completed a hat-trick of wins in 1999. Not only that, but they won the double twice in both 1997 and 1999. After finishing four points clear of Gorica in the league last term they beat old rivals Olimpija 5–2 on aggregate in the two-leg cup final.

Maribor made their European debut in the 1992–93 Cup-winners' Cup. They had an easy start in the preliminary round against Hamrun Spartans of Malta. Ante Simundza, who remains Maribor's most dangerous forward, scored their first two goals in international competition in a 4–0 win. Maribor went through 5–2 on aggregate, but then crashed out 9–1 overall to Atletico Madrid.

Another nine-goal thrashing awaited them in the UEFA Cup first round in 1997–98 when Maribor were crushed in Amsterdam by Ajax. Turning the tables, Maribor themselves smashed 10 goals without reply past Norma Tallinn of Estonia in the 1994–95 Cup-winners' Cup qualifying round. However, until this season, their modest boast at international level was to have reached merely the second round of the UEFA Cup back in 1993.

Ante Aimundza: Maribor's most-dangerous forward.

Speed on the counter-attack is the secret weapon with which Maribor hoped to maintain their surprisingly successful Champions League progress. But they also rely heavily on the reflexes and sure handling of Slovenia international goalkeeper, Marko Simeunovic.

He played the game of his life in the first qualifying round against Genk. Maribor won the first leg 5–1, but were then losing 3–0 in the return and had been reduced to 10 men by the expulsion of defender Amir Karic. Somehow Simeunovic managed to reach everything Genk could throw at him and Maribor survived.

Coach Bojan Prasnikar has proved over the years, with both the national team and with Olimpija Ljubljana, to be a devotee of the 3-5-2 tactical system. The 29-year-old Marinko Galic is a reliable sweeper with Dejan Djuranovic, Croatia's Stipe Balajic and Simon Seslar the engine room in central midfield. Simundza – Maribor's all-time European top scorer before this season with seven goals – and Kliton Bozgo hunt together in attack. Bozgo is one of Maribor's five foreign players. Born and brought up in Albania, he holds Slovene citizenship through marriage.

Lyon manager Bernard Lacombe has great respect for Maribor now – and wishes his players had paid more attention to his warnings before their tie. Lacombe says, admiringly: "Maribor are a team any opponent has to take seriously. They are very fit and their spirit is excellent. They know they are underdogs, but they go out determined to defy anybody who comes up against them."

Even from the land of the World Cup holders.

Maribor Records

European honours: None

Record European victory: 10–0 v Norma Tallinn, Cup-winners' Cup qualifying round 1994–95

Record European defeat: 0–9 v Ajax, UEFA Cup 1st round 1997–98

Club records: Herbert Klancnik (411 matches), Branko Horjak (103 goals)

Record attendance: 15,500 (v HNK Hajduk Split in old stadium)

Formed 1891 **Coach** Stuart Baxter **Stadium** Rasunda
Capacity 36,800 **Address** Box 1408, 171 27 Solna
Website www.aik.se

AIK Solna

AIK have been the great Swedish domestic soccer success story of the 1990s – their revivalist glory mirroring the re-emergence of the national team as an international force.

The decade has seen Sweden rebuild their reputation with progress to the semi-finals of both the 1994 World Cup and 1992 European Championship. Sweden were also one of the first teams to secure their place in the finals of Euro 2000.

AIK have reflected that international success at domestic level – as befits one of Sweden's oldest sporting institutions.

The club were founded on February 15, 1891, their name an abbreviation for Allmanna Idrottsklubben, which means General Sports Club. Athletics was supposed to be the main sport, with the soccer section not being launched until 1896 – but it quickly became the most important.

AIK won their first domestic championship – then a knock-out competition – in 1900 and were founder members of the league in 1924. They were one of the most successful clubs though not always the most popular. The team's traditional ability to gnaw out a result earned them the nickname of "*gnagare*" or "rodents." It did not help their reputation that the club's traditional black shirts tended to fade to a rat-like grey after steady visits to the laundry!

Now the successors to those original "rodents" are maintaining the club's proud traditions.

AIK have won the league championship 10 times and the cup on seven occasions down the years. But the 1990s probably represents their finest era with two league championships and three cup wins.

AIK have yet, however, to succede at European level. They first ventured abroad in 1965, but lost to Servette of Switzerland in the second round of the old Fairs Cup. In 11 attempts the club had never progressed beyond the second round in any of the cups until 1996–97, when AIK fell to Barcelona in the Cup-winners' Cup quarter-final.

Thus this season's entry into the Champions League group stages represented their finest achievement so far – a real feather in the cap for coach Stuart Baxter.

The 46 year-old from Wolverhampton had enjoyed a modest professional career as a winghalf with Preston North End, Dundee and Stockport County. Then he embarked on an international Odyssey which has reached a pinnacle with AIK in the Champions League. His cv includes playing then coaching as far afield as Australia (South Melbourne Hellas), Cyprus (Halkanoras Dali), Portugal (Vitoria Setubal) and Japan (winning the J.League

Pontus Kamark: back in Sweden after his success in England.

with Sanfrecce Hiroshima).

But it is Swedish players who appear to respond best to his working style.

Goalkeeper Mattias Asper, for example, set a Swedish record this year of 796 minutes without conceding a goal. His magic spell was finally broken in early September when AIK lost 1–0 to IFK Gothenburg. It was a rare defeat which came only days before AIK opened their Champions League group campaign against Barcelona.

In front of Asper, the centre of AIK's defence has been built around Michael Brundin, whose ability to read a game makes up for the fact that, at 33, he is considered a veteran in football terms.

Baxter generally deploys a 4-4-2 formation secured on the anchor of experienced Pontus Kamark. Now 30, Kamark returned to Sweden last year after a successful spell in English football with unfashionable Leicester City. Kamark's most notable role was in Leicester's 1997 League Cup victory over Middlesbrough, when he man-marked Brazilian star Juninho out of the game.

Another of Sweden's prodigal sons is forward Andreas Andersson. He first hit the Champions League headlines with IFK Gothenburg, so impressing Italian giants Milan with his performances against them that they signed him in mid-season. But Milan were entering a difficult era with a quick turnover in both coaches and players and Andersson moved to England with Newcastle United – again finding himself at a club in turmoil.

Now both he and AIK have the chance to develop both their confidence and their reputation.

AIK Solna Records

European honours: None

Record European victory: 8–0 v Red Boys Differdange, Cup-winners' Cup, 1985–86

Record European defeat: 2–5 v Hannover 96, Fairs Cup, 1968–69

Club records: Gustav Sjoberg (321 league matches), Par Kaufeldt (124 league goals)

Record scorer in Europe: Pascal Simpson, 7

Record attendance: 40,669 (v Djurgardens IF, 1975)

Squad List

No.	Name	Date of birth	Position	Nationality	Domestic apps/goals	European Cup apps/goals
1	Matthias ASPER	20.03.1974	Goalkeeper	Sweden	39 / 0	4 / 0
12	Lee BAXTER	17.06.1976	Goalkeeper	England	7 / 0	0 / 0
23	Niklas WESTBERG-ANDERSSON	01.04.1979	Goalkeeper	Sweden	0 / 0	0 / 0
26	Alexander VALENTINI	13.10.1981	Goalkeeper	Sweden	0 / 0	0 / 0
3	Karl CORNELIUSSON	17.11.1976	Defender	Sweden	69 / 3	3 / 1
5	Michael "BRUNTE" Brundin	05.10.1965	Defender	Sweden	158 / 0	12 / 1
6	Tomas GUSTAFSSON	07.05.1973	Defender	Sweden	70 / 1	6 / 1
15	David LJUNG	27.09.1975	Defender	Sweden	19 / 0	4 / 0
16	Mike KJOLO	27.10.1971	Defender	Norway	44 / 2	4 / 0
17	Pontus KAMARK	05.04.1969	Defender	Sweden	149 / 4	32 / 1
20	Patric ENGLUND	28.12.1965	Defender	Sweden	136 / 11	6 / 0
27	Robert WENNBERG	21.01.1981	Defender	Sweden	0 / 0	0 / 0
2	Krister "KRILLE" Nordin	25.02.1968	Midfielder	Sweden	273 / 47	24 / 1
4	Ola ANDERSSON	01.07.1966	Midfielder	Sweden	78 / 2	10 / 0
8	Daniel TJERNSTROM	19.02.1974	Midfielder	Sweden	154 / 17	8 / 1
9	Hans BERGH	06.06.1970	Midfielder	Sweden	120 / 5	0 / 0
14	Thomas LAGERLOF	15.11.1971	Midfielder	Sweden	159 / 8	14 / 0
18	Marcus BENGTSSON	29.01.1979	Midfielder	Sweden	1 / 0	0 / 0
21	Andreas JOHANSSON	05.07.1978	Midfielder	Sweden	44 / 6	0 / 0
22	Benjamin KIBEBE	13.08.1981	Midfielder	Sweden	0 / 0	0 / 0
24	Stefan ISHIZAKI	15.05.1982	Midfielder	Sweden	0 / 0	0 / 0
7	Nebojsa "NESCHO" Novakovic	29.10.1964	Forward	Sweden	110 / 25	8 / 2
10	Martin ASLUND	10.11.1976	Forward	Sweden	85 / 6	3 / 0
11	Andreas ANDERSSON	10.04.1974	Forward	Sweden	82 / 48	13 / 2
13	Christer MATTHIASSON	29.07.1971	Forward	Sweden	68 / 34	2 / 0
19	Daniel HOCH	11.05.1979	Forward	Sweden	9 / 2	1 / 0

Formed 1886 **Coach** Arsene Wenger **Stadium** Wembley **Capacity** 80,000 **Address** Arsenal Stadium, Highbury, London N5 1BU **Website** www.arsenal.co.uk

Arsenal

FOURTH time lucky for Highbury's Gunners? Arsenal won the Fairs/UEFA Cup in 1970 and the Cup-winners' Cup in 1994. They reached Cup-winners' Cup finals in 1980 and 1995, too, but London's most-famous club has yet to make an impression in the European Cup, or Champions League.

Dennis Bergkamp: the inspiration behind the London club.

Arsenal's best run came in 1971–72, when they lost 1–3 on aggregate to holders Ajax in the quarter-finals.

In 1991–92, Arsenal failed to reach the first-ever Champions League stage. A first-round demolition of FK Austria was followed by an extra-time home exit to Benfica. Last season, defeats by Kiev and Lens saw off the Gunners at the qualifying stage.

"Not done ourselves justice, have we?" said skipper Tony Adams, a veteran of those last two campigns. Now Adams believes Arsenal are equipped to compete at this exalted level. "The difference is our strength in depth," he says: "We didn't have that last season."

In the summer of 1998, Arsene Wenger made only one major signing, the Argentina full back, Nelson Vivas. Non-flying Dennis Bergkamp was ruled out of the games in both Kiev and Athens (against Panathinaikos). Arsenal's only forward cover was Chris Wreh and the even less experienced Luis Boa Morte.

Since then, Wenger has signed Swedish winger Fredrik Ljungberg, Nigerian striker Nwankwo Kanu from Inter, right back Oleh Luzhnyi from Kiev, midfielder Stefan Malz (TSV Munich 1860) and the Brazilian left back Silvinho.

On the brink of the new season, he added two forwards, Davor Suker and Thierry Henry, to replace the eternal malcontent Nicolas Anelka, banished to Real Madrid for £23 million.

Arsenal Records

European honours: Cup-winners' Cup 1993–94, Fairs Cup 1969–70

Record European victory: 7–0 v Standard Liege, Cup-winners' Cup, 1993–94

Record European defeat: 1–5 v Spartal Moscow, UEFA Cup 1982–83

Club records: David O'Leary (772 first-class matches), Ian Wright (185 goals)

Record scorer in Europe: Ian Wright, 15

Record attendance (Wembley): 126,047 (April 28th, 1923)

Wenger said: "Suker lives for goals. He has to do some work to get match fit, but he will be a great asset to us." Everyone who saw Suker destroy Aston Villa at Highbury will testify to the quality of his finishing. Can he maintain that consistency?

Henry's finishing is the biggest question mark against him. Wenger said: "He gives us many more options. He has pace and he can play on either flank, or through the middle." But when Arsenal beat Bradford City 2–0 and Bergkamp seemed determined to create a goal for him, Henry did not score.

The draw though, was kind to Bergkamp. He could be chauffeur-driven to Florence, Barcelona and Stockholm, all approximately two-day journeys.

The one thing Arsenal lack in attack though is aerial power – unless Adams strides forward for a dead-ball move.

In midfield, Patrick Vieira and Manu Petit (injured for a month after a 0–0 draw at Sunderland) are the heartbeat of the team. Ray Parlour on the right contributes so much energy. The stability they provide enables Marc Overmars to cut in and score the goals that have become his trademark.

The ever-shrewd Wenger has studiously avoided predictions; beyond the obvious at least. "I think we're in the toughest group of the lot," he said. "The expansion of the Champions League has created so many more games. There are too many now. I will have to rotate our squad much more than last season, because the number of matches makes things very hard for the players."

Arsenal's first three games included trips to Fiorentina and Barcelona. Adams had a target in mind: "We have to make sure we're still in contention by the end of the opening phase. We know we can't leave ourselves too much to do."

Steve Bould's move to Sunderland broke up the renowned Arsenal back four. Adams believes Bould's experience could have come in handy – though the Gunners' skipper sees 20-year-old Matthew Upson as his long-term successor. But Adams' partnership with Martin Keown – which stretches back to the 1982 Arsenal youth team – will be crucial to their chances.

So will the absence of red and yellow cards. Wenger knows his team must improve their disciplinary record. Last season, Vieira, Manu Petit, Nigel Winterburn, Bergkamp, Lee Dixon and Parlour all got into trouble with referees.

Arsenal also have to make the most of playing in front of 70,000-plus crowds at Wembley. The pitch is bigger. There is more space. The famous setting inspires the visitors. That was all said last year. Now the Gunners know what to expect.

"The draw is tough but exciting," said Adams: "Beautiful cities, great stadiums, terrific atmosphere. We're rarin' to go."

Squad List

No.	Name	Date of birth	Position	Nationality	Domestic apps/goals	European Cup apps/goals
1	**David SEAMAN**	19.09.1963	Goalkeeper	England	619 / 0	34 / 0
13	**Alex MANNINGER**	04.06.1977	Goalkeeper	Austria	20 / 0	2 / 0
24	**John LUKIC**	11.12.1960	Goalkeeper	England	593 / 0	9 / 1
2	**Lee DIXON**	17.03.1964	Defender	England	571 / 31	31 / 0
3	**Nigel WINTERBURN**	11.12.1963	Defender	England	581 / 16	33 / 0
5	**Martin KEOWN**	24.07.1966	Defender	England	459 / 7	21 / 1
6	**Tony ADAMS**	10.10.1966	Defender	England	524 / 31	29 / 3
7	**Nelson David VIVAS**	18.10.1969	Defender	Argentina	24 / 0	5 / 0
16	**SILVINHO**	12.04.1974	Defender	Brazil	7 / 0	0 / 0
18	**Gilles GRIMANDI**	11.11.1970	Defender	France	33 / 1	15 / 0
22	**Oleg LUZHNYI**	05.08.1968	Defender	Ukraine	1 / 0	52 / 0
4	**Patrick VIEIRA**	23.06.1976	Midfielder	France	105 / 8	12 / 1
8	**Fredrik LJUNGBERG**	16.04.1977	Midfielder	Sweden	21 / 2	9 / 0
15	**Ray PARLOUR**	07.03.1973	Midfielder	England	212 / 17	17 / 0
17	**Emmanuel PETIT**	22.09.1970	Midfielder	France	62 / 6	42 / 1
19	**Stefan MALZ**	15.06.1972	Midfielder	Germany	0 / 0	3 / 0
20	**Stephen HUGHES**	18.09.1976	Midfielder	England	47 / 4	5 / 1
23	**Alberto MENDEZ**	24.10.1974	Midfielder	Germany	4 / 0	1 / 0
31	**Paolo VERNAZZA**	01.11.1979	Midfielder	England	3 / 0	1 / 0
33	**Greg LINCOLN**	23.03.1980	Midfielder	England	0 / 0	0 / 0
9	**Davor SUKER**	01.01.1968	Forward	Croatia	4 / 2	23 / 10
10	**Dennis BERGKAMP**	10.05.1969	Forward	Holland	126 / 53	39 / 21
11	**Marc OVERMARS**	29.03.1973	Forward	Holland	74 / 18	46 / 5
12	**Christopher WREH**	14.05.1975	Forward	Liberia/France	30 / 3	10 / 1
14	**Thierry HENRY**	17.08.1977	Forward	France	7 / 0	24 / 8
21	**Jermaine PENNANT**	15.01.1977	Forward	England	0 / 0	0 / 0
25	**Nwankwo KANU**	01.08.1976	Forward	Nigeria	18 / 8	22 / 1

Formed 1899 **Coach** Louis Van Gaal **Stadium** Estadi FC Barcelona (Nou Camp) **Capacity** 98,109 **Address** Aristides Maillol s/n, 08028 Barcelona **Website** www.fcbarcelona.es

Barcelona

BARCELONA are a historic and record-breaking club. There are no other words for it. They were the first-ever Spanish league champions in 1929 and share the honour of never having been relegated from the Spanish first division with Real Madrid and Athletic Bilbao. They boast the largest number of members of any European club with 102,000 and a recent survery by accountancy firm Deloitte and Touche made Barcelona the richest club in continental Europe.

Their magnificent home, Nou Camp, has staged the opening match of the World Cup finals (in 1982), the Olympic Games final (in 1992) and finals of all the three European club competitions – the Champions Cup (most memorably last season when Manchester United snatched overtime victory over Bayern Munich with goals from Sheringham and Solskjaer), the Cup-winners' Cup and the UEFA/Fairs Cup.

But, for all the achievement, Barcelona are always controversial – most notably for the manner in which Dutch coach, Louis Van Gaal, has taken advantage of the Bosman ruling to surround himself with a flock of his fellow countrymen. Dutch stars out on the pitch include the De Boer twins,

Squad List

No.	Name	Date of birth	Position	Nationality	Domestic apps/goals	European Cup apps/goals
1	Ruud HESP	31.10.1965	Goalkeeper	Holland	75 / 0	21 / 0
25	Francesc ARNAU	23.03.1975	Goalkeeper	Spain	2 / 0	0 / 0
2	Michael REIZIGER	03.05.1973	Defender	Holland	57 / 0	38 / 0
5	ABELARDO Fernandez	19.04.1970	Defender	Spain	306 / 21	30 / 3
12	SERGI Barjuan Esclusa	28.12.1971	Defender	Spain	200 / 4	43 / 2
17	Winston BOGARDE	22.10.1970	Defender	Holland	21 / 2	25 / 1
3	Frederic DEHU	24.10.1972	Defender	France	2 / 0	11 / 1
22	Frank DE BOER	15.05.1970	Defender	Holland	20 / 2	71 / 1
4	Josep GUARDIOLA	18.01.1971	Midfielder	Spain	216 / 3	52 / 2
15	Philip COCU	29.10.1970	Midfielder	Holland	38 / 12	33 / 5
21	Luis Enrique MARTINEZ	08.05.1970	Midfielder	Spain	289 / 74	49 / 6
26	Xavi HERNANDEZ CREUS	25.01.1980	Midfielder	Spain	17 / 1	6 / 0
6	Ronald DE BOER	15.05.1970	Midfielder	Holland	14 / 0	54 / 6
10	Jari LITMANEN	20.02.1971	Midfielder	Finland	0 / 0	48 / 25
20	SIMAO Sabrosa	31.10.1979	Midfielder	Portugal	0 / 0	4 / 0
7	Luis FIGO	04.11.1972	Forward	Portugal	142 / 22	44 / 6
11	RIVALDO Vitor Borba Ferreira	19.04.1972	Forward	Brazil	114 / 66	14 / 4
14	Emmanuel AMUNIKE	25.12.1970	Forward	Nigeria	19 / 1	9 / 0
19	DANI Garcia Lara	22.12.1974	Forward	Spain	117 / 21	19 / 9
23	Boudewijn ZENDEN	15.08.1976	Forward	Holland	26 / 0	13 / 2
28	Gabriel Garcia de la Torre, GABRI	10.02.1979	Forward	Spain	2 / 0	0 / 0
9	Patrick KLUIVERT	01.07.1976	Forward	Holland	37 / 16	24 / 10
30	NANO	20.04.1982	Forward	Spain	1 / 0	0 / 0

Barcelona Records

European honours: European Cup 1991–92; Cup-winners' Cup 1978–79, 1981–82, 1988–89, 1996–97; Fairs Cup 1957–58, 1959–60, 1965–66

Record European victory: 8–0 v Apollon Limassol, Cup-winners' Cup 1st round 1982–83

Record European defeat: 2–6 v Valencia, Fairs Cup Final 1961–62

Club records: Miguel "Migueli" Bernardo Bianqueti (656 matches), Paulino Alcántara (356 goals)

Record scorer in Europe: Evaristo, 27

Record attendance: 120,000 (v Juventus FC, March 5th, 1986)

Ronald and Frank, Phillip Cocu, Winston Bogarde, Michael Reiziger, goalkeeper Ruud Hesp, Boudewijn Zenden and Patrick Kluivert.

The reward was immediate – Van Gaal's Barcelona won the league and cup double in 1998 for the first time in 39 years.

Now, as they come to the end of their centenary year, Barcelona's eyes are fixed on emulating their old domestic enemies, Real Madrid, and regaining the Champions League Cup.

It would, of course, mark their second such success, having won the cup in 1992 under Johan Cruyff, beating Sampdoria 1–0 after extra time at Wembley to make up for the disappointment of losing the 1986 final in Spain to underdogs Steaua Bucharest after then-coach, Terry Venables, had led them to their first domestic league title in 11 years.

Barca have also won the now-defunct Cup-winners' Cup four times, the last of which was three years ago when Paris Saint-Germain were the victims, and the old Fairs Cup three times.

If anyone is to lead them back to the European Cup-winning glory then few coaches could boast a better pedigree than Van Gaal.

Now 48, Amsterdam-born Van Gaal was a respected player in the 1970s with Ajax, Antwerp (Belgium), Telstar, Sparta and AZ'67 Alkmaar. But his playing career pales into insignificance beside his coaching achievements.

After retiring prematurely, he was promoted from assistant to senior coach of Ajax in September 1991 in succession to Leo Beenhakker (now with Feyenoord). Van Gaal had previously been assistant to Beenhakker and wasted no time in bringing a fresh approach to the side. He has also delivered a major honour in each of his five seasons in charge. Under Van Gaal Ajax won the UEFA Cup in 1992, the Dutch cup in 1993, the league championship in 1994, 1995 and 1996 and … the Champions Cup in 1995 when Ajax beat Milan 1–0 in Vienna.

Now he tries to lead another group of Dutchmen – albeit flavoured with the Brazilian genius of Rivaldo – to a similar triumph.

Rivaldo: the Brazilian genius poses an ever-present threat.

Formed 1926 **Coach** Giovanni Trapattoni **Stadium** Stadio Comunale Artemio Franchi **Capacity** 47,350 **Address** Piazza Girolamo Savanarola 6, 50132 Firenze **Website** www.acfiorentina.it

Fiorentina

FIORENTINA'S president, Vittorio Cecchi Gori, is not one for cautious optimism, when bravura will do. But when Cecchi Gori says the Viola are on the brink of building a "legendary team", it's not just enthusiasm running away with him.

Fiorentina beat Poland's Widzew Lodz 3–1 at home and 2–0 away to ease into a Champions League place. It is the first time they have taken part in Europe's premier club competition since they won the "scudetto" in 1969.

The Viola finished third in Serie A last season, after leading for the early part of the campaign. A knee injury to leading scorer, Gabriel "Batigol" Batistuta, effectively wrecked their title hopes.

Fiorentina – and legendary coach Giovanni Trappatoni – have taken steps to avoid a repeat. Trappatoni, the former international wing half, is the most successful coach in Italian club history. Now he wants to add a major honour with the Viola.

Edmundo's summer return to Brazil relaxed the tension in the dressing room – and provided "Trap" with extra cash to spend. Fiorentina's first target was Parma's Enrico Chiesa.

Squad List

No.	Name	Date of birth	Position	Nationality	Domestic apps/goals	European Cup apps/goals
1	**Francesco TOLDO**	02.12.1971	Goalkeeper	Italy	169 / 0	14 / 0
12	**Giuseppe TAGLIATELA**	02.01.1969	Goalkeeper	Italy	162 / 0	6 / 0
22	**Gianmatteo MAREGGINI**	08.01.1967	Goalkeeper	Italy	82 / 0	0 / 0
2	**Tomas REPKA**	02.01.1974	Defender	Czech	33 / 0	26 / 0
3	**Moreno TORRICELLI**	23.01.1970	Defender	Italy	184 / 3	52 / 2
4	**Daniele ADANI**	10.07.1974	Defender	taly	53 / 3	1 / 2
5	**Pasquale PADALINO**	26.07.1972	Defender	Italy	181 / 11	9 / 0
6	**Aldo FIRICANO**	12.03.1967	Defender	Italy	252 / 12	17 / 2
17	**Jorg HEINRICH**	06.12.1969	Defender	Germany	35 / 4	27 / 3
23	**Alessandro PIERINI**	22.03.1973	Defender	Italy	103 / 6	5 / 0
27	**Andrea TAROZZI**	17.10.1973	Defender	Italy	70 / 0	3 / 0
36	**Giacomo BONORA**	11.02.1980	Defender	Italy	0 / 0	0 / 0
7	**Guillermo AMOR**	04.12.1967	Midfielder	Spain	16 / 0	63 / 11
10	**Cesar Manuel RUI COSTA**	29.03.1972	Midfielder	Portugal	158 / 28	21 / 6
11	**Fabio ROSSITTO**	21.09.1971	Midfielder	Italy	152 / 4	0 / 0
13	**Luigi PAGLIUCA**	29.08.1979	Midfielder	Italy	0 / 0	0 / 0
14	**Sandro COIS**	09.06.1972	Midfielder	Italy	173 / 7	18 / 2
15	**Paul OKON**	05.04.1972	Midfielder	Australia	21 / 0	11 / 0
16	**Angelo DI LIVIO**	26.07.1966	Midfielder	Italy	189 / 3	51 / 1
21	**Mauro BRESSAN**	05.01.1971	Midfielder	Italy	131 / 2	1 / 0
24	**Christian AMOROSO**	22.09.1976	Midfielder	Italy	45 / 0	5 / 0
31	**Ricardo TADDEI**	05.09.1980	Midfielder	Italy	0 / 0	0 / 0
35	**Roberto MUSSO**	17.06.1980	Midfielder	Italy	0 / 0	0 / 0
8	**Pedrag MIJATOVIC**	19.01.1969	Forward	Yugoslavia	2 / 0	32 / 7
9	**Gabriel Omar BATISTUTA**	01.02.1969	Forward	Argentina	214 / 129	12 / 5
18	**Abel Eduardo BALBO**	01.06.1966	Forward	Argentina	232 / 114	24 / 10
20	**Enrico CHIESA**	29.12.1970	Forward	Italy	182 / 71	20 / 17

Then the Viola decided they should sign two forwards instead of one.

So Fiorentina spent £5.5 million on Predrag Mijatovic from Real Madrid, before adding Chiesa.

Mijatovic, scorer of Real's winner against Juventus in the 1998 Champions League final, agreed a three-year contract. At first, Chiesa seemed happier to stay with Parma, but coach Alberto Malesani (once of Fiorentina) wanted to re-structure his attack. Faustino Asprilla was off-loaded to Palmeiras, and Parma won the race for Serie A's leading scorer last season, Udinese's 22-goal Brazilian, Marcio Amoroso. Parma paid £22 million for the privilege, and then shelled out £6.5 million for Marco Di Vaio from Salernitana.

So Chiesa finally arrived in Florence – gift-wrapped at £11million – to sign a four-year deal that could see him through to the end of his career. "He's very quick, with an impressive scoring record," said Trappatoni, maybe dreaming of the 22 Serie A goals Chiesa netted for Sampdoria in 1995–96, before his move to Parma.

"Batigol", meanwhile, has been recovering from persistent problems in his left knee, which flared up again after the Viola's victory over Lodz. He has been at Stadio Artemio Franchi since 1991, even taking a one-season excursion into Serie B when Fiorentina were relegated. Such loyalty from overseas imports is rare, let alone in the cash-crazy world of calcio. In 1995, Batistuta equalled the legendary Swede Kurt Hamrin's record of 26 goals for Fiorentina in a Serie A season. With 144 goals to Hamrin's 150, "Batigol" is poised to break the Swede's all-time record.

"Even on one leg, I always like him on the pitch," said Trappatoni.

After two such big-name signings, Cecchi Gori was beaming. "I always said we'd get the best players for the best deals – and I keep my promises," said the Viola president.

The trick now is for Trappatoni to make them all perform. "Trap" likes to play 3-4-3. Batistuta, it seems, will operate as the advanced striker, with Mijatovic and Chiesa playing off him.

That means a new role for playmaker Rui Costa. Previously he broke from midfield to support the attack, bursting into the space created by Batistuta's runs. He can't do that, with Mijatovic and Chiesa ahead of him. "Trap" wants him to play the midfield general.

Gabriele Batistuta: the Argentinian forward has been with the club since 1991 – such loyalty is rare nowadays.

"Rui Costa will be Rui Costa," smiled Trappatoni. "But he'll be running around a bit less and directing operations a bit more. At 27, he's the right age for it." First, he has to convince the Portuguese international.

Sandro Cois, as ever, will be the midfield anchor, with Jorg Heinrich raiding from wing back.

Meanwhile, other less-specatacular signings, may be equally important to the Viola's progress. The veteran Juventus midfielder, Angelo Di Livio, may turn out to be one of the bargains of the season, at just over £1 million. Brescia's Daniele Adani (£2.5 million) and Alessandro Pierini (£3.8 million from Udinese) give "Trap" options in the back three, alongside Pasquale Padalino and the Czech, Tomas Repka.

With Anselmo Robbiati joining Napoli and back-up striker Carmine Esposito moving to Sampdoria, Trappatoni snapped up yet another forward, 33-year-old Abel Balbo, also from Parma and still a lethal poacher.

"The Champions League is special for us. We have a lot of players with the right sort of experience," said Trappatoni. "We could have had a less demanding draw. There are definitely easier groups. On the other hand, prestige teams like Barcelona and Arsenal will bring out the best in us. The Champions League should be a stimulus to our season.

"And we're stronger now than we were this time last year."

Fiorentina Records

European honours: Cup-winners' Cup 1960–61

Record European victory: 6–2 v Lucerne, Cup-winners' Cup quarter-final 1960–61; 6–2 v Rapid Vienna, Cup-winners' Cup 2nd round 1961–62

Record European defeat: 2–6 v Anderlecht, UEFA Cup 2nd round 1984–85

Club records: Giancarlo Antognoni (341 matches), Kurt Hamrin (151 goals)

Record scorer in Europe: Kurt Hamrin, 15

Record attendance: 58,217 (v Internazionale, November 11th, 1984)

Formed 1903 **Coach** Jaime Pacheco **Stadium** Estadio do Bessa **Capacity** 13,000 **Address** Rua o Primeiro de Janeiro, 4100 Porto **Website** None

Boavista

BOAVISTA are one of the surprise contenders for the Champions League – competing in the premier European club event for the first time in their history.

Until this year Boavista had been overshadowed by the achievements of their city neighbours, FC Porto. Then, for only the second time in their 96 years, they came within a dream of carrying off the Portuguese league title.

It would have been the first time in 53 years that a club from outside the "Big Three" of Porto, Benfica and Sporting had won the title. But history was not to be. In the end Boavista finished eight points behind Porto, but runners-up spot was more than enough to promote them into the Champions League.

Until now Boavista had always taken great pride in their exploits in the Portuguese cup, which they won five times between 1975 and 1997. But coach Jaime Pacheco, a former international midfielder who took over midway through the 1997–98 term, had greater ambitions for the club.

He says: "For a small club like ours, the Champions League is a golden opportunity both to earn a lot of money and to gather experience against some of the finest teams in Europe. Maybe we can strike a few blows for small clubs everywhere.

"Certainly my players will not be overawed by the challenge. Our players have been well prepared physically and mentally for whatever match we have to play, in whatever competition and against whoever the opponents. My players are very proud and excited about playing in the Champions League and knowing that the whole of Europe will be watching them. We could even be the surprise team of our group. We have great faith in our own abilities."

Boavista's surge has been founded on a secure defence. Cameroon's William Andem was perhaps the outstanding goalkeeper in the Portuguese league last season while the playmaking skills of Romanian midfielder, Ion Timofte, made Porto fans wonder why their club had ever let him join their neighbours.

Timofte, who won the league with Porto, amazed even himself by finishing last season as Boavista's joint top scorer on 15 goals alongside Ghanaian striker, Ayew. Indeed, Timofte boasts a scoring ratio of one goal every three

William Andem: last season's outstanding keeper in Portugal.

Squad List

No.	Name	Date of birth	Position	Nationality	Domestic apps/goals	European Cup apps/goals
1	**RICARDO Pereira**	11.02.1976	Goalkeeper	Portugal	55 / 0	2 / 0
12	**Bassey WILLIAM Andem**	14.06.1968	Goalkeeper	Cameroon	33 / 0	2 / 0
24	**PEDRO ALBERGARIA**	12.12.1980	Goalkeeper	Portugal	0 / 0	0 / 0
2	**PAULO SOUSA**	31.03.1967	Defender	Portugal	249 / 0	22 / 0
4	**SERGIO Pereira de Carvalho**	06.05.1977	Defender	Portugal	0 / 0	0 / 0
5	**PEDRO EMANUEL Silva**	11.02.1975	Defender	Portugal	65 / 1	8 / 0
14	**CARLOS ALBERTO Ribeiro Pereira**	10.10.1974	Defender	Brazil	0 / 0	0 / 0
15	**William QUEVEDO**	08.05.1971	Defender	France	52 / 3	2 / 0
17	**Carlos Manuel Magalhaes "LITOS"**	25.02.1974	Defender	Portugal 1	39 / 10	8 / 2
21	**JORGE SILVA**	04.12.1975	Defender	Portugal	0 / 0	1 / 0
30	**MARIO SILVA**	24.04.1977	Defender	Portugal	25 / 1	8 / 1
3	**RUI BENTO**	14.01.1972	Midfielder	Portugal	209 / 3	29 / 2
6	**PEDRO Rui Mota MARTINS**	17.07.1970	Midfielder	Portugal	144 / 9	14 / 0
7	**Ion TIMOFTE**	16.12.1967	Midfielder	Romania	200 / 61	21 / 4
8	**LUIS MANUEL Viana**	06.11.1970	Midfielder	Portugal	154 / 8	2 / 0
13	**EMANUEL Braga**	07.07.1975	Midfielder	Portugal	84 / 7	1 / 0
27	**Antonio Jose FORMOSO**	08.02.1974	Midfielder	Portugal	74 / 8	7 / 0
9	**GILMAR Estevan**	11.04.1967	Forward	Brazil	158 / 48	13 / 3
10	**Almani Samori MOREIRA**	16.06.1978	Forward	Portugal	0 / 0	2 / 1
11	**CESAR Atienza**	14.07.1975	Forward	Spain	0 / 0	0 / 0
16	**Joaquim Pereira Silva "MARTELINHO"**	19.11.1974	Forward	Portugal	0 / 0	6 / 0
18	**Rudolph DOUALA Mbela**	25.09.1978	Forward	Cameroon	26 / 5	0 / 0
19	**Jose ROGERIO De Melo**	03.10.1974	Forward	Portugal	0 / 0	0 / 0
20	**JORGE COUTO**	01.07.1970	Forward	Portugal	220 / 21	29 / 2
22	**RICARDO Fernandes SILVA**	29.03.1977	Forward	Portugal	6 / 0	0 / 0
23	**AUGUSTINE Ahinful**	30.11.1974	Forward	Ghana	16 / 6	8 / 3
26	**WHELLITON Augusto da Silva**	23.07.1972	Forward	Brazil	0 / 0	1 / 0

matches which is remarkable for any midfielder, let alone one from one of the country's less fashionable sides.

Other bargain signings from FC Porto who have gained a new lease of life with Boavista include international forward, Jorge Couto. He has vast experience of European club competition with more than 30 matches to his name. He is also one of Boavista's most consistent stars, having made nearly 250 league appearances in the Portuguese top division down the years.

But Boavista are not a club with a big transfer budget, nor are they foolish enough to plunge into debt for the sake of a big name or two. Instead they study the market in players whom Pacheco believes have a special skill to suit the team.

Thus one-time Sporting Lisbon cast-off, Luis Manuel, is the anchor man in the centre of midfield, while the attack has been strengthened for the Champions League campaign by the acquisitions of Brazilian Gilmar Estevan from Vitoria Guimaraes and Ghana forward Augustine Ahinful from the Italian club Venezia. They are among nine foreign players in the Boavista squad.

Pacheco believes these new men will more than make amends for the summer departures of Ayew – to Sporting – defender Helder and midfielder Isaias. Indeed, Augustine was quick to prove the point with a decisive goal in the qualifying round victory over Danish club, Brondby.

Whatever the outcome of the Champions League season, Boavista will take away the satisfaction of having shared in a piece of competition history. This is the first season that two clubs from the same city have competed in the event since the introduction of the group structure: Boavista and FC Porto share that honour with London's Arsenal and Chelsea.

Boavista Records

European honours: None

Record European victory: 8–0 v Sliema Wanderers, Cup-winners' Cup 1st round 1979–80

Record European defeat: 0–5 v Lazio, UEFA Cup 1st round 1977–78

Club records: Pedro Barbosa (334 matches), Jose Antonio Calado (64 goals)

Record scorer in Europe: Artur, 7

Record attendance: 18,500 v FC Porto, November 15, 1992

Formed 1909 **Coach** Michael Skibbe **Stadium** Westfalenstadion **Capacity** 68,600 (52,000 intls) **Address** Westfalenstadion, Strobelallee, Postfach 100509, 44005 Dortmund **Website** www.borussia-dortmund.de

Borussia Dortmund

BORUSSIA Dortmund know what it is like to triumph in the world's most prestigious international club event. That is why rebuilding has been such a painful process over the past two years.

Dortmund shocked Europe when they defeated favourites Juventus 3–1 in the 1997 Champions League Final. The fact that the greatest night in Dortmund's history was celebrated in the home stadium of old rivals Bayern Munich was an added bonus.

The problem for Dortmund was the need for massive change in both coaching and playing personnel in the succeeding months. Ottmar Hitzfeld, who had guided Dortmund to glory, decided to move "upstairs" and new Italian coach, Nevio Scala, struggled to get to grips with German football – or, at least, struggled to convince Dortmund's impatient fans.

A string of injuries added to the confusion and Scala was replaced by little-known youth coach, Michael Skibbe. Despite initial misgivings among media and fans, that choice has been vindicated with Dortmund's return this season to the Champions League.

Dortmund were German pioneers in Europe. In fact,

Squad List

No.	Name	Date of birth	Position	Nationality	Domestic apps/goals	European Cup apps/goals
1	**Jens LEHMANN**	10.11.1969	Goalkeeper	Germany	216 / 2	20 / 0
12	**Wolfgang DE BEER**	02.01.1964	Goalkeeper	Germany	178 / 0	10 / 0
2	**Christian WORNS**	10.05.1972	Defender	Germany	232 / 0	23 / 1
3	**Karsten BAUMANN**	14.10.1969	Defender	Germany	250 / 9	4 / 0
5	**Jurgen KOHLER**	06.10.1965	Defender	Germany	321 / 26	65 / 5
6	**Wolfgang FEIERSINGER**	30.01.1975	Defender	Austria	50 / 0	36 / 2
7	**Stefan REUTER**	16.10.1966	Defender	Germany	383 / 25	73 / 7
15	**Alfred NIJHUIS**	23.03.1966	Defender	Holland	150 / 15	2 / 0
32	**Jorg SAUERLAND**	24.12.1976	Defender	Germany	2 / 0	0 / 0
4	**Miroslav STEVIC**	07.01.1970	Midfielder	Yugoslavia	176 / 9	8 / 0
8	**Christian NERLINGER**	21.03.1973	Midfielder	Germany	182 / 28	34 / 6
9	**Vladimir BUT**	07.09.1977	Midfielder	Russia	57 / 7	11 / 1
10	**Andreas MOLLER**	02.09.1967	Midfielder	Germany	317 / 102	61 / 20
14	**Sergei BARBAREZ**	17.09.1971	Midfielder	Bosnia-Herzegovina	82 / 17	1 / 0
16	**Sead KAPETANOVIC 2**	1.01.1972	Midfielder	Bosnia-Herzegovina	48 / 2	0 / 0
17	**Leonardo DE DEUS SANTOS (Dede)**	18.04.1978	Midfielder	Brazil	32 / 0	2 / 0
18	**Lars RICKEN**	10.07.1976	Midfielder	Germany	130 / 18	34 / 8
19	**Otto ADDO**	09.06.1975	Midfielder	Ghana/Germany	0 / 0	0 / 0
23	**EVANILSON Aparecido Ferreira**	12.09.1975	Midfielder	Brazil	1 / 0	0 / 0
11	**Heiko HERRLICH**	03.12.1971	Forward	Germany	213 / 62	27 / 8
13	**Giuseppe REINA**	15.04.1972	Forward	Italy/Germany	67 / 14	1 / 0
20	**Fredi BOBIC**	30.10.1971	Forward	Germany	151 / 70	13 / 9
22	**Ibrahim TANKO**	25.07.1977	Forward	Ghana	40 / 3	11 / 0
24	**Viktor IKPEBA**	12.06.1973	Forward	Nigeria	3 / 0	38 / 14

they became the first German club to win a European trophy when they beat Liverpool 2–1 in extra time in the Cup-winners' Cup Final in Hampden Park, Glasgow, in 1966. Right winger "Stan" Libuda scored a sensational winning goal with a lob from way out on the right touchline. A few weeks later, no fewer than three Dortmund players – goalkeeper Hans Tilkowski and forwards Sigi Held and Lothar Emmerich – were starring in the West German side who finished World Cup runners-up to England at Wembley.

Dortmund, who have won the league championship on five occasions and the cup twice, play their home matches in the Westfalen stadium which was built for the 1974 World Cup. UEFA regulations which prohibit standing areas and bench seats in international competition explain why the stadium's Champions League capacity is reduced.

Still, Dortmund's volatile and voluble fans fill the stadium for just about every big game and provide the atmosphere within which their international stars can flourish.

Andreas Moller: vast experience of the big occasion.

Andreas Moller is perhaps the most famous. A member of the German World Cup-winning squad in Italy in 1990, he has been one of his country's most-dominant and most-controversial personalities ever since. Moller has vast experience of the big occasion – having also won the UEFA Cup during a spell in Italian football with Juventus – and the pinpoint accuracy of his free kicks and corners is legendary. It was Moller's corners which created two of Dortmund's European Cup-winning goals against Juventus in 1997.

That Dortmund have rebuilt with such evident success is especially remarkable since they have been without attacking sweeper Matthias Sammer for virtually all this time. Sammer was a key man both when Germany won the 1996 European Championship in England and then with Dortmund in the Champions League a year later. But a serious knee injury has sidelined him ever since and he has been prevented, by a succession of complications, from returning to big-match action.

At least Dortmund's defensive security has been maintained thanks to the presence of Stefan Reuter and Jurgen Kohler. Both are veterans of the 1990 World Cup win and the 1997 Champions League victory and both rank among Europe's most experienced defenders. Indeed, Kohler was long considered the finest stopper in the business anywhere in the international game.

Dortmund spent more than £14 million during the summer, investing some of their assured income from the Champions League in new players to strengthen Skibbe's hand. Out went veteran German midfielder Thomas Hassler and Swiss striker Stephane Chapuisat and in came defensive midfielder Christian Worns, Nigerian World Cup playmaker Victor Ikpeba and German international centre-forward Fredi Bobic.

Coach Skibbe has set the quarter-finals as a minimum target. Dortmund certainly have the talent to go that far. Whether they can emulate the class of '97 is another matter.

Borussia Dortmund Records

European honours: European Cup 1996–97; Cup-winners' Cup 1995–96

Record European victory: 8–0 v Floriana Valletta, Cup-winners' Cup 1st round 1965–66

Record European defeat: 1–6 v Manchester United, Fairs Cup 2nd round 1964–65

Club records: Michael Zorc (463 Bundesliga matches), Manfred Burgsmuller (135 Bundesliga goals)

Record scorer in Europe: Stephane Chapuisat, 16

Record attendance: 68,600 (capacity occasions)

Formed 1908 **Coach** Leo Beenhakker **Stadium** De Kuip
Capacity 51,177 **Address** Olympiaweg 50, 3077 AL Rotterdam
Website www.feyenoord-fanpage.nl

Feyenoord

FEYENOORD, in the early 1960s, were considerd one of the richest clubs in Europe – if not the richest. Their potential for wealth and power was underlined in 1970 when they became the first Dutch club to win the European Champions Cup.

Jon Dahl Tomasson: the Dane is just one of a number of attacking options.

Later they added the UEFA Cup to the trophy shelves in Rotterdam. But later years were not all as happy – which is why the current European campaign is so important from both financial and sporting perspectives.

Feyenoord's star was eclipsed in Europe by old rivals Ajax Amsterdam, but the record books show that they have won the Dutch league title 15 times and the cup 10 times – second only to Ajax in both competitions.

Feyenoord were founded in 1918 by the mining entrepreneur C.R.J. Kieboom. Their star player in the successful pre-war years was left half, Puck Van Heel, who appeared in the finals tournaments of both the 1934 and 1938 World Cups and set what was for many years a Dutch record of 64 international appearances.

The post-war years were bleak until after the introduction of professionalism in the late 1950s. Then Feyenoord entered their most glorious domestic era, winning the league title in 1961, 1962, 1965, 1969, 1971 and 1974. Indeed, their 1965 and 1969 successes brought them league and cup doubles.

Stars in defence were goalkeeper Eddie Pieters Graafland, a then-record £20,000 signing from Ajax, as well as skipper and rightback Gerard Kerkum and the halfback line of Reinier Kreyermaat, Hans Kraay (later club manager) and Jan Klaasens.

Inspiration in attack was provided by left winger Coen Moulijn. He was still a key figure, though approaching the veteran stage, when Feyenoord made their international breakthrough in 1970, alongside Swedish striker Ove Kindvall and midfield general Wim Van Hanegem. Feyenoord's coach, for their extra-time victory over Celtic in Milan in 1970, was former Austrian international Ernst Happel.

Certainly the football style with which Ajax subsequently dominated Europe – total football – brought the Amsterdam club a showering of praise and glory during the golden years of the 1970s, yet it was Feyenoord who were the first Dutch club to break through the international competitive barrier, not only in the Champions Cup, but also in the World Club Cup (again in 1970). Feyenoord beat Argentina's Estudiantes in a rough, tough, two-leg final.

But, as time went on, Feyenoord lost their grip on the Dutch game. Ajax and then PSV Eindhoven dominated the prizes and Feyenoord's crowds began to fade. Star players were sold to balance the books.

A series of boardroom and managerial changes culminated in the return to the club of Wim Jansen – the 1974 World Cup midfielder – as manager. He raised morale and the later appointments of old favourite Van Hanegem as coach further extended the Feyenoord revival. Then, last season, under Leo Beenhakker, Feyenoord regained the league title for the first time in six years and only the second time in the 1990s.

Jurek Dudek is goalkeeping successor to the traditions of Pieters Graafland and Ed De Goey (now with Chelsea), while Bert Konterman, Ulrich Van Gobbel and Kees Van Wonderen are stalwarts in defence. The midfield is guided by skipper Jean-Paul Van Gastel and Feyenoord boast a mixture of attacking styles and skills through Denmark's Jon Dahl Tomasson, Ivory Coast's Bonaventure Kalou and their Argentine top scorer, Julio Cruz.

It is a measure of the extent to which the Champions League responds to so many financial and business influences that Feyenoord coach Beenhakker believes this season's winners will not be coming from Rotterdam, but from Italy, Spain or England.

He says: "Expanding the Champions League suits the biggest clubs who need to prevent early elimination, because of the financial consequences that would bring. Certainly then, the winning club will be Italian, English or Spanish. It's simple economics: these are countries whose clubs have the biggest budgets."

Feyenoord Records

European honours: European Cup 1969–70; UEFA Cup 1973–74

Record European victory: 12–0 v Rumelange, UEFA Cup 1st round 1972–73

Record European defeat: 0–5 v Real Madrid, European Cup 1st round 1965–66

Club records: Coen Moulin (487 matches), Cor van der Gijp (161 goals)

Record scorer in Europe: Lex Schoenmaker, 19

Record attendance: 65,427 (v FC Twente, December 22nd, 1968)

Squad List

No.	Name	Date of birth	Position	Nationality	Domestic apps/goals	European Cup apps/goals
1	Jerzy "Jurek" DUDEK	23.03.1973	Goalkeeper	Poland	72 / 0	10 / 0
21	Edwin ZOETEBIER	7.05.1970	Goalkeeper	Holland	221 / 0	0 / 0
25	Cor VARKEVISSER	14.05.1982	Goalkeeper	Holland	0 / 0	0 / 0
26	Ronald GRAAFLAND	30.04.1979	Goalkeeper	Holland	0 / 0	0 / 0
2	Chris GYAN	02.11.1978	Defender	Ghana	28 / 1	2 / 0
3	Tomasz RZASA	11.03.1973	Defender	Poland	54 / 4	4 / 0
4	Bernard SCHUITEMAN	03.10.1973	Defender	Holland	84 / 2	21 / 0
8	Kees Van WONDEREN	04.01.1969	Defender	Holland	139 / 8	14 / 2
15	Patricio GRAFF	18.11.1975	Defender	Argentina	44 / 1	12 / 0
16	Bert KONTERMAN	14.01.1971	Defender	Holland	159 / 15	2 / 0
20	Ferry De HAAN	12.09.1972	Defender	Holland	9 / 0	1 / 0
22	Ulrich Van GOBBEL	16.01.1971	Defender	Holland	217 / 8	32 / 0
23	Mohammed ALLACH	20.09.1973	Defender	Holland	0 / 0	0 / 0
27	Steve OLFERS	25.02.1982	Defender	Holland	0 / 0	0 / 0
5	Jean-Paul Van GASTEL	28.04.1972	Midfielder	Holland	236 / 37	17 / 8
6	Paul BOSVELT	26.03.1970	Midfielder	Holland	217 / 43	12 / 0
17	Patrik PAAUWE	27.12.1975	Midfielder	Holland	120 / 11	2 / 0
19	Jan De VISSER	01.01.1968	Midfielder	Holland	201 / 15	4 / 1
28	Thomas BUFFEL	19.02.1981	Midfielder	Belgium	0 / 0	0 / 0
7	Bonaventure KALOU	12.01.1978	Forward	Ivory Coast	44 / 10	2 / 0
9	Julio Ricardo CRUZ	10.10.1974	Forward	Argentina	59 / 33	8 / 3
10	Jon Dahl TOMASSON	29.08.1976	Forward	Denmark	114 / 51	10 / 2
11	Radoslav SAMRDZIC	17.10.1970	Forward	Yugoslavia	120 / 38	4 / 1
13	Ronildo Pereira de Freitas "TININHO"	23.10.1977	Forward	Brazil	29 / 1	1 / 0
14	Peter Van VOSSEN	21.04.1968	Forward	Holland	75 / 13	30 / 4
18	Igor KORNEEV	04.09.1967	Forward	Russia	74 / 15	10 / 2
24	Wanderson DE PAULA "SOMALIA"	22.06.1976	Forward	Brazil	0 / 0	0 / 0

Formed 1917 **Coach** Nils Arne Eggen **Stadium** Lerkendal Stadion **Capacity** 24,779 **Address** Boks 4126, 7002 Trondheim **Website** www.rbk.no

Rosenborg Trondheim

ROSENBORG Trondheim are one of the most consistent competitors in the Champions League. That is a remarkable boast to emanate from Norway, which has never been considered a member of the European football jet set.

Yet Rosenborg compete for the fifth successive season and, for the first time, by well-earned right as one of the elite batch of 16 top-seeded clubs. Not for Rosenborg, this year, the pressure of coming up through the qualifying rounds. Rosenborg's achievements, in recent years, earned them an automatic key to the door.

Rosenborg are a prime example of the manner in which the fall-out from the advent of the UEFA Champions League is reaching right down into the domestic game. Rosenborg's mere presence in the Champions League – even before bonus money for wins and draws – is highly profitable. Thus the club do not have to worry unduly about foreign predators luring away their star players.

The answer is simple: Rosenborg are so well-off, thanks to the Champions League, that they can buy whatever players they want from anywhere else and from any other club in Norway. Such a transfer policy not only keeps Rosenborg strong, but it keeps their domestic rivals weak – and subject to Rosenborg's domination both on and off the pitch.

The proof is in the record books. Rosenborg came into the 1999–2000 Champions League having won the last seven Norwegian championships and apparently well on the way towards yet another. In that time they have also won the cup – and thus the double – twice. Five times in these one-sided seasons a Rosenborg striker has finished as the league's top scorer.

Squad List

No.	Name	Date of birth	Position	Nationality	Domestic apps/goals	European Cup apps/goals
1	**Jorn JAMTFALL**	24.07.1966	Goalkeeper	Norway	151 / 0	28 / 0
12	**Arni Gautur ARASON**	07.05.1975	Goalkeeper	Iceland	11 / 0	2 / 0
24	**Espen ISAKSEN**	16.01.1979	Goalkeeper	Norway	0 / 0	0 / 0
2	**Andre BERGDOLMO**	13.10.1971	Defender	Norway	102 / 5	30 / 1
3	**Erik HOFTUN**	03.03.1969	Defender	Norway	218 / 14	38 / 1
4	**Bjorn Otto BRAGSTAD**	05.01.1971	Defender	Norway	252 / 27	38 / 1
5	**Christer BASMA**	01.08.1972	Defender	Norway	46 / 1	10 / 0
14	**Ole Johan SIGNSDAL**	08.05.1979	Defender	Norway	0 / 0	0 / 0
22	**Lasse STRAND**	03.04.1974	Defender	Norway	3 / 0	0 / 0
6	**Roar STRAND**	02.02.1970	Midfielder	Norway	287 / 61	44 / 11
7	**Orjan BERG**	20.08.1968	Midfielder	Norway	90 / 14	11 / 0
10	**Bent Andre SKAMMELSRUD**	18.05.1966	Midfielder	Norway	290 / 59	46 / 5
15	**Mads Kristian SKJAERVOLD**	03.01.1980	Midfielder	Norway	1 / 0	0 / 0
19	**Fredrik Guttormsen WINSNES**	28.12.1975	Midfielder	Norway	68 / 4	6 / 0
20	**Bent Inge JOHNSEN**	28.01.1972	Midfielder	Norway	31 / 8	8 / 4
8	**Jan Derek SORENSEN**	28.12.1971	Forward	Norway	60 / 22	12 / 4
9	**John CAREW**	05.09.1979	Forward	Norway	3 / 3	6 / 4
11	**Jahn Ivar 'Mini' JAKOBSEN**	08.11.1965	Forward	Norway	276 / 137	35 / 8
13	**Thor Hogne AAROY**	20.03.1977	Forward	Norway	0 / 0	0 / 0
16	**Arne WINSNES**	27.04.1974	Forward	Norway	6 / 0	0 / 0
18	**Oyvind STORFLOR**	18.12.1979	Forward	Norway	1 / 0	0 / 0
21	**Tore Andre DAHLUM**	21.06.1968	Forward	Norway	133 / 55	17 / 1

Roar Strand: a member of the seemingly telepathic midfield trio.

Harald Brattbakk was leading marksman three years in a row from 1994 with 17 then 26 and 28 goals. He was followed, both in the Rosenborg attack and in top spot in the league scoring charts by Siggi Rushfeldt, who totalled 25 goals in 1997 and 27 in 1998.

Coach Nils Arne Eggen's long-established tactical base – to suit whoever is coming or going at Rosenborg – is 4-3-3. Norway international Jarn Jamtfall is the experienced goalkeeper with Christer Basma, Erik Hoftun, Bjorn Otto Bragstad and Andre Bergdolmo a solid back line. Roar Strand, Bent Skammelsrud and Orjan Berg appear to virtually read each other's minds as they interchange in midfield and John Carew is the new sharpshooter up front since Rushfeldt's mid-summer sale to Benfica.

Yet Rosenborg's rise is a recent phenomenon. Although the club were founded in 1917, they did not become a significant force in Norwegian, let alone Scandinavian. club football until the early 1960s. The enthusiastic ambition of a hard-core group of ambitious supporters coincided with the arrival of one of the greatest of Norwegian football personalities – Odd Iversen (father of Tottenham striker Steffen Inversen).

The greatest domestic goalscorer in the history of the Norwegian game joined Rosenborg in 1962, midway between their breakthrough cup victories of 1960 and 1964.

Rosenborg won the league title for the first time in 1967 with Iversen the championship's leading marksman on 17 goals. He also scored in the cup final that season, but Rosenborg's dream of their first double was shattered by a 4–1 defeat at the hands of Lyn from Oslo.

The club won the league again in 1969 and, though Iversen left to try his luck in professional football in Belgium, the impetus he had helped established proved enduring. The first, elusive, league-and-cup double was achieved in 1971 and Roseborg now boast two decades of solid-gold success.

Rosenborg have been leaders among the move towards professionalism in Norwegian football, benefiting from strong local support with league crowds averaging an excellent 12,000. They play all their home matches in the municipally owned Lerkendal stadium.

The Lerkendal once drew its biggest crowds for athletics events. Not any longer.

Rosenborg Trondheim Records

European honours: None

Record European victory: 6–0 v Grevenmacher, UEFA Cup qualifying round 1994–95

Record European defeat: 0–9 v Hibernian, UEFA Cup 1st round 1974–75

Club records: Ola By Rise (457 matches), Odd Iversen (158 goals)

Record scorer in Europe: Harald Brattback, 14

Record attendance: 28,455 (v Lillestrom SK, October 1985)

Formed 1906 **Coach** Osvaldo Ardiles **Stadium** Maksimir Stadium **Capacity** 38,000 **Address** Maksimirska 128, 10 000 Zagreb **Website** www.nk-croatia.com

Croatia Zagreb

CROATIA Zagreb have been loyal supporters of European international club football for more than 30 years, but events far beyond boundaries of the football pitch have conspired to give the club a new identity.

Robert Prosinecki: back in Croatia with a point to prove.

As Dinamo Zagreb, within the confines of the former Yugoslavia, Croatia first appeared on the scene as far back as 1958, when the entire concept of international competition was a novelty. Then, in the original Champions Cup, they were first-round losers to Dukla Prague. Over the next 20 years, however, they missed only a handful of seasons in one competition or another.

More than that, Dinamo Zagreb became one of the first eastern European sides to win a European trophy when they defeated Leeds United in the final of the 1967 Fairs Cup.

In those days Dinamo relied entirely on home-grown players. Now, renamed NK Croatia as a defiant symbol of independence since the crisis of the early 1990s, the club have a very different outlook.

Now they look abroad not for only players, but for coaches as well – such as present boss, Osvaldo Ardiles, who was appointed this past summer. Few modern players can claim a more cosmopolitan football background than Ardiles, who was playmaker of the Argentina side who won the 1978 World Cup as hosts, then starred in England with Tottenham Hotspur before turning to management first in England (with Swindon, Newcastle United and Tottenham Hotspur) before moving to Japan.

Pressure is intense. Croatian fans have a high opinion of their football and great expectations – particularly since the national squad, featuring six players from the Croatia club finished third in the 1998 World Cup finals in France. Also, the Croatia club have won the league championship in five of the eight seasons since independence as well as the domestic on four occasions and the league-and-cup double three times.

Ardiles, who had been desperate to return to Europe to prove himself after some unfortunate experiences in England with Tottenham, Newcastle and Swindon, has been under no illusion about the size of the challenge. He has to make Croatia a force in European club football while maintaining their domestic domination.

After a comparatively sluggish start to the domestic season he admitted: "It began to feel as if someone was asking me about my job security almost every week. But when you become a coach you have to learn to accept

Squad List

No.	Name	Date of birth	Position	Nationality	Domestic apps/goals	European Cup apps/goals
1	**Drazen LADIC**	01.01.1963	Goalkeeper	Croatia	748 / 0	39 / 0
12	**Tomislav BUTINA**	30.03.1974	Goalkeeper	Croatia	88 / 0	1 / 0
23	**Vladimir VASILJ**	06.07.1975	Goalkeeper	Croatia	12 / 0	0 / 0
2	**Mario TOKIC**	23.07.1975	Defender	Croatia	58 / 0	10 / 0
3	**Damir KRZNAR**	10.07.1972	Defender	Croatia	191 / 18	13 / 1
4	**Goce SEDLOSKI**	10.04.1974	Defender	Macedonia	11 / 0	10 / 1
5	**Goran JURIC**	05.02.1963	Defender	Croatia	115 / 0	30 / 0
17	**Mario CVITANOVIC**	06.05.1975	Defender	Croatia	158 / 9	11 / 0
20	**Stjepan TOMAS**	06.03.1976	Defender	Croatia	150 / 1	12 / 0
6	**Zoran PAVLOCIC**	27.06.1976	Midfielder	Croatia	– / –	5 / 1
7	**Nermin SABIC**	21.12.1973	Midfielder	Bosnia-Herzegovina	57 / 3	3 / 0
8	**Robert PROSINECKI**	12.01.1969	Midfielder	Croatia	93 / 34	48 / 14
10	**Edin MUJCIN**	14.01.1970	Midfielder	Bosnia-Herzegovina	182 / 40	20 / 3
11	**Tomislav RUKAVINA**	14.10.1974	Midfielder	Croatia	160 / 18	18 / 2
21	**Josko JELICIX**	05.01.1971	Midfielder	Croatia	210 / 81	15 / 3
22	**Igor BISCAN**	04.05.1978	Midfielder	Croatia	74 / 10	5 / 0
24	**Krunoslav JURCIC**	26.11.1969	Midfielder	Croatia	151 / 9	16 / 0
25	**Tomo SOKOTA**	08.04.1977	Midfielder	Croatia	93 / 31	7 / 0
30	**Niljenko MUMLEK**	21.11.1972	Midfielder	Croatia	– / –	9 / 6
9	**Grazvidas MIKULENAS**	16.12.1973	Forward	Lithuania	21 / 9	15 / 2
14	**Mihael MIKIC**	06.01.1980	Forward	Croatia	46 / 14	5 / 1
15	**Daniel SARIC**	04.08.1972	Forward	Croatia	185 / 26	21 / 3
16	**Josip SIMIC**	16.09.1977	Forward	Croatia	66 / 27	9 / 3
18	**Mario BAZINA**	08.09.1975	Forward	Croatia	– / –	0 / 0
26	**Adrian KOZNIKU**	27.10.1969	Forward	Croatia	28 / 10	10 / 3

that pressure – and the further up the game you go the greater that pressure. But we have a great club and it's normal that our supporters are always expecting us to win.

"When I first talked to the club president he told me what he wants from this season: he wants to win the championship of Croatia, he wants changes in the team and more quality in our play. So we're playing under great pressure of our own making and we know we don't have a God-given right to win. Not even Barcelona win all their games."

The quality control challenge was one which Ardiles welcomed. He says: "In a way we are in show business. People buy the tickets – and they are not cheap – and we must entertain them."

Creating a team who can both entertain and win is a task which has eluded many of the most experienced coaches. At least Ardiles had a head start with the quality he found already in the Croatia squad.

The favoured tactic of both coach and players is 3-5-2, with Drazen Ladic a confidence-inspiring goalkeeper behind a defensive trio anchored by Goran Juric. Ahead of them is a versatile midfield who look to experienced Robert Prosinecki to turn defence into rapid-fire attack.

Prosinecki began his career in the old Dinamo days. He even played for the former Yugoslavia in the 1990 World Cup finals, then won a Champions Cup medal with Red Star Belgrade a year later. He was considered Europe's finest new talent and was soon lured to Spain. His seasons with Real Madrid and Barcelona were marred by injuries, but a return to Croatia has offered him a welcome new chance to shine – even if winning the Cup itself is beyond the club's realistic hopes.

Croatia Zagreb Records

European honours: Fairs Cup 1966–67 (as Dinamo Zagreb)

Record European victory: 7–2 v Copenhagen, Fairs Cup 1st round 1961–62

Record European defeat: 1–5 v Barcelona, Fairs Cup 2nd round 1961–62

Club records: Drazen Ladic (760 matches), Igor Cvitanovic (104 goals)

Record scorer in Europe: Igor Cvitanovic, Slaven Zambata, 14

Record attendance: 63,000 (v Santos in 1963)

Formed 1902 **Coach** Sir Alex Ferguson **Stadium** Old Trafford **Capacity** 56,024 **Address** Sir Matt Busby Way, Old Trafford, Manchester M16 0RA **Website** www.manutd.com

Manchester United

HOW do you follow the treble? That's the question Manchester United have to answer this season. They also have the little matter of the World Club Championship to attend to in January.

The late goals – by subs Teddy Sheringham and Ole Gunnar Solskjaer – that destroyed Bayern in Barcelona earned United boss Alex Ferguson a knighthood and proved that a Premiership club could win the European Cup.

Sir Alex acknowledges that winning it again may be an even tougher task, especially with the fixture demands on the club.

"The hardest job will be to retain the European Cup, because of the number of games now involved – 17 if you go all the way," he said. "We also have to go to Tokyo for the Intercontinental Cup, and then to Brazil for the World Club Championship."

Sir Alex hopes United will be on course for the Champions League quarter-finals when they journey to Brazil, but he is concerned at the possible effects of the trip. "It worries me, the heat of the afternoon, the kick-off times demanded by European television. I'm mindful of our players' exertion at the hottest time of the year in Brazil."

But the holders looked well placed to qualify from a group completed by Marseille, Croatia Zagreb and the Austrian outsiders Sturm Graz.

"We enjoy playing in Europe because European nights always have a fantastic atmosphere," said Sir Alex, who believes Barcelona could pose the most formidable danger to United. "They have bought well during the summer and look a big threat," he said.

Ironically, before United's 1990 FA Cup final replay win over Crystal Palace, sections of the Old Trafford crowd were calling for Sir Alex's head – though they probably don't remember that now. That Wembley victory took the pressure off Sir Alex and enabled him to build his dynasty at United.

His contribution has been heroic – not least in the early re-organisation of United's scouting and youth policy. How that has paid dividends. The Neville brothers, Ryan Giggs, Paul Scholes, Nicky Butt and David Beckham have all risen through Old Trafford's youth ranks. Sir Alex was brave enough to give them their chance – even when pundits like Alan Hansen insisted: "You'll win nothing with kids." United's

Dwight Yorke: made an immediate impact on United.

Manchester United Records

European honours: European Cup 1967–68, 1998–99; Cup-winners' Cup 1990–91

Record European victory: 10–0 v Anderlecht, European Cup 1st round 1956–57

Record European defeat: 0–5 v Sporting Lisbon, Cup-winners' Cup quarter-final 1963–64

Club records: Bobby Charlton (606 matches and 199 goals in the league)

Record scorer in Europe: Denis Law, 28

Record attendance: 70,504 (v Aston Villa, December 27th, 1920)

success since 1995–96 has proved the perfect answer.

Arsene Wenger often says that English managers are judged by the players they recruit. If that is the case Sir Alex is a genius, too.

Take the summer of 1998. Arsenal had won the "double". United, league runners-up, had won nothing. Sir Alex went signing. In came Jaap Stam, Jesper Blomqvist and Dwight Yorke.

Stam has proved the massive centre back presence United have lacked since the days of Gary Pallister and Steve Bruce. He has started the new season in majestic form. Swedish winger Blomqvist gives United options on either flank, and allows Sir Alex to move Giggs inside at will.

Signing Yorke was a master-stroke. Venerated by the Holte End faithful at Aston Villa, Yorke was just the man United needed to partner Andy Cole. He scored 18 goals in the championship and eight in the Champions League. At £12.6 million, he seemed like a snip, such was the impact he made.

United's biggest worry has been replacing Peter Schmeichel, who played his last game for them in the European Cup final.

Schmeichel's replacement, Mark Bosnich has been troubled by injury. The £4.5 million signing of Massimo Taibi from Venezia suggested that Bosnich had not convinced the Old Trafford coaching staff – though UEFA ruled Taibi ineligible for the first set of group matches. That left the job between Bosnich and the club's goalkeeping coach 36-year-old Raimond Van der Gouw, who stood in for Bosnich at the start of the season.

Injuries have hit United's defenders, too. Cruciate ligament damage will keep young defender Wes Brown out for months. Ronny Johnsen also has serious knee problems. Gary Neville is only just returning after a groin injury. David May has also been sidelined. Phil Neville and Henning Berg will take important roles while United wait for their colleagues to recover.

But Sir Alex prefers to play in the other team's half and United's attacking prowess is exceptional. Roy Keane remains the midfield dynamo. Beckham provides magnificent crosses and telling dead-ball kicks. Giggs can dribble opponents off the pitch.

Sir Alex can also call on the combative Nicky Butt, or the finishing power of Paul Scholes, depending on the balance he wants in central midfield.

Up front, the Dwight Yorke-Andy Cole combo will test Europe's best defences again. And Sir Alex has Sheringham and Solskjaer in reserve. "I've got four strikers who've all contributed brilliantly," he said.

That's one of United's greatest virtues, though – strength in depth throughout the squad. Just ask Bayern.

Squad List

No.	Name	Date of birth	Position	Nationality	Domestic apps/goals	European Cup apps/goals
1	**Mark BOSNICH**	13.01.1972	Goalkeeper	Australia	185 / 1	11 / 0
17	**Raimond VAN DER GOUW**	24.03.1963	Goalkeeper	Holland	14 / 0	18 / 0
2	**Gary NEVILLE**	18.02.1975	Defender	England	150 / 2	35 / 0
3	**Denis IRWIN**	31.10.1965	Defender	Ireland	614 / 24	46 / 3
4	**David MAY**	24.06.1970	Defender	England	202 / 9	12 / 1
6	**Jaap STAM**	17.07.1972	Defender	Holland	37 / 1	23 / 0
12	**Philip NEVILLE**	21.01.1977	Defender	England	109 / 1	18 / 1
13	**John CURTIS**	03.09.1978	Defender	England	13 / 0	0 / 0
21	**Henning BERG**	01.09.1969	Defender	Norway	209 / 5	19 / 1
23	**Michael CLEGG**	03.07.1977	Defender	England	9 / 0	1 / 0
24	**Wesley BROWN**	13.10.1979	Defender	England	20 / 0	4 / 0
7	**David BECKHAM**	02.05.1975	Midfielder	England	156 / 31	33 / 5
8	**Nicky BUTT**	21.01.1975	Midfielder	England	146 / 13	32 / 0
11	**Ryan GIGGS**	29.11.1973	Midfielder	Wales	260 / 54	33 / 10
14	**Jordi CRUYFF**	09.02.1974	Midfielder	Holland	26 / 4	16 / 0
15	**Jesper BLOMQVIST**	05.02.1974	Midfielder	Sweden	24 / 1	25 / 6
16	**Roy KEANE**	10.08.1971	Midfielder	Ireland	271 / 33	28 / 6
18	**Paul SCHOLES**	16.11.1974	Midfielder	England	130 / 34	27 / 7
25	**Quinton FORTUNE**	21.05.1977	Midfielder	South Africa	0 / 0	0 / 0
32	**Mark WILSON**	09.02.1979	Midfielder	England	13 / 4	1 / 0
9	**Andy COLE**	15.10.1971	Forward	England	268 / 151	25 / 15
10	**Teddy SHERINGHAM**	02.04.1966	Forward	England	476 / 193	11 / 3
19	**Dwight YORKE**	03.11.1971	Forward	Trinidad & Tobago	270 / 96	20 / 10
20	**Ole Gunnar SOLSKJAER**	26.02.1973	Forward	Norway	77 / 36	25 / 6
22	**Erik NEVLAND**	10.11.1977	Forward	Norway	1 / 0	0 / 0
34	**Jonathan GREENING**	02.01.1979	Forward	England	28 / 2	0 / 0

Formed 1899 **Coach** Rolland Courbis **Stadium** Stade Velodrome **Capacity** 60,000 **Addresss** 25 rue Negresko, BP 124, 13267 Marseille Cedex 08 **Website** www.olympiquedemarseille.com

Marseille

MARSEILLE have been on a roller-coaster ride ever since they won the Champions Cup in 1993.

Robert Pires: skipper and fulcrum of the team.

Basile Boli's glancing header that beat AC Milan in Munich launched the biggest celebrations in the club's history. But, after revelations of a match-fixing scandal, the French federation relegated "l'OM" to the second division and UEFA suspended them from European competition for a season. Club president Bernard Tapie was disgraced and jailed.

Now Marseille have risen again. They have always been one of the wealthiest and best-supported clubs in France. The crowd at the Velodrome is probably the most passionate in French football. The gigantic blue and white banner – "*Fiers d'être marseillais*" (proud to be from Marseille) – draped around the front of the home end says it all.

Those fans' expectations are huge. Marseille have won both the French championship and the cup 10 times. Last season, they finished runners-up to Bordeaux in the league and lost to Parma in the final of the UEFA.

Indiscipline did not help their cause, however, Christophe Dugarry, Fabrizio Ravanelli, full back William Gallas and midfielder Peter Luccin were all suspended for the showdown.

Dugarry, one of France's 1998 World Cup-winning squad, was not expecting to enter the Champions League action until the fifth game of the first group phase. He was suspended for fighting in the UEFA Cup semi-final against Bologna last season and, on top of that, suffered knee trouble which needed surgery.

Marseille's massive support expected big signings before the

Marseille Records

European honours: European Cup 1992–93

Record European victory: 7–1 v Union Luxembourg, UEFA Cup 1st round 1973–74

Record European defeat: 0–5 v Sporting Lisbon, UEFA Cup 2nd round 1973–74

Club records: Roger Scotti (360 matches), Gunnar Andersson (169 goals)

Record scorer in Europe: Jean-Pierre Papin, 23

Record attendance: 57,603 (v Paris Saint-Germain, April 8th, 1998)

Champions League campaign. There have been plenty of arrivals at the Velodrome, but also a significant departure in the transfer to Internazionale of influential sweeper Laurent Blanc.

"You can't stop a 34 year-old like Laurent wanting a last challenge with Ronaldo and Christian Vieri," said Marseille coach Rolland Courbis. Argentine sweeper Eduardo Berizzo arrived from River Plate to cover for Blanc. It took him time to adjust, but his partnership with the towering South African international Pierre Issa may prove crucial to Marseille's solidity.

Experienced 31-year-old Patrick Blondeau gives the coach another option, but Courbis, nevertheless, recalled Daniel Montenegro from a loan spell with Argentine club Huracan to maintain defensive strength in depth.

Gallas and ex-Blackburn left back Sebastian Perez are the other markers in front of fast-improving young goalkeeper Stephane Porato – though Perez's natural tendency is to fly into attack. That is where Stephane Dalmat may come in handy. When l'OM paid Lens £7 million for the defensive midfielder this summer, it was a record for a deal between French clubs. Courbis sees Dalmat as Marseille's box-to-box man, capable of protecting his back line one moment, then instantly breaking forward. But with Robert Pires – and a fit Ivan de la Pena – alongside him, Dalmat is likely to spend more time defending than attacking.

Pires – another of France's World Cup-winning squad – is the fulcrum of the team, a roving midfielder who makes chances and takes them. The Olympique skipper is likely to push up behind the front men. Meanwhile Courbis hopes De la Pena – "the little Buddha" – can finally shake off a series of muscle injuries to create from further back. De la Pena, once of Barcelona, rarely had the chance to shine at Lazio and joined Marseille on loan in the summer.

Courbis changes Marseille's formation according to circumstances. In tight away games, he often opts for a fourth midfielder in the harrying mould. At home, though, Courbis often uses three strikers. Italian Fabrizio Ravanelli has Champions League-winning experience from his days with Juventus, while Florian Maurice is a top-class predator and Ibrahima Babayoko a far more dangerous raider than his spell at Everton suggested.

As the legendary Marseille and France centre back Marius Tresor says: "Marseille are at their strongest when they take the game to the opposition. They have players who can score at the highest level. And they're very strong at home. The Velodrome is an intimidating arena for visitors ..."

Squad List

No.	Name	Date of birth	Position	Nationality	Domestic apps/goals	European Cup apps/goals
1	**Stephane PORATO**	12.09.1973	Goalkeeper	France	57 / 0	7 / 0
16	**Stephane TREVISAN**	01.05.1973	Goalkeeper	France	4 / 0	0 / 0
30	**Laurent SPINOSI**	20.12.1969	Goalkeeper	France	– / –	0 / 0
2	**Patrick BLONDEAU**	27.01.1968	Defender	France	182 / 2	34 / 1
3	**Sebastien PERZ**	24.11.1973	Defender	France	134 / 14	6 / 1
4	**Pierre ISSA**	11.09.1975	Defender	South Africa	31 / 0	7 / 1
5	**Lilian MARTIN**	28.05.1971	Defender	France	43 / 0	13 / 1
6	**Eduardo BERIZZO**	16.11.1969	Defender	Argentina	5 / 0	0 / 0
20	**Richard MARTINI**	26.08.1978	Defender	France	– / –	0 / 0
23	**William GALLAS**	17.08.1977	Defender	France	56 / 0	9 / 0
24	**Yannick FISCHER**	17.12.1974	Defender	France	145 / 2	6 / 0
8	**Frederic BRANDO**	08.11.1973	Midfielder	France	173 / 6	11 / 0
10	**Ivan DE LA PENA**	06.05.1976	Midfielder	Spain	1 / 0	20 / 3
12	**Stephane DALMAT**	16.02.1979	Midfielder	France	58 / 4	5 / 0
14	**Djamel BELMADI**	25.03.1976	Midfielder	France	6 / 1	0 / 0
17	**Seydou KEITA**	16.01.1980	Midfielder	Mali	0 / 0	0 / 0
18	**Daniel Gaston MONTENEGRO**	28.03.1979	Midfielder	Argentina	– / –	12 / 0
26	**Peter LUCCIN**	09.04.1979	Midfielder	France	83 / 1	12 / 0
27	**Jacques ABARDONADO**	25.05.1978	Midfielder	France	– / –	0 / 0
7	**Robert PIRES**	29.10.1973	Forward	France	202 / 49	20 / 3
9	**Florian MAURICE**	20.01.1974	Forward	France	192 / 66	23 / 8
11	**Fabrizio RAVANELLI**	11.12.1968	Forward	Italy	54 / 23	43 / 21
15	**Pablo Ignacio CALANDRIA**	15.03.1982	Forward	Argentina	0 / 0	0 / 0
19	**Kaba DIAWARA**	16.12.1975	Forward	France	77 / 17	8 / 0
21	**Christophe DUGARRY**	24.03.1972	Forward	France	202 / 37	38 / 12
22	**Ibrahima BAKAYOKO**	31.12.1976	Forward	Ivory Coast	81 / 26	2 / 0
25	**Arthur MOSES**	03.03.1973	Forward	Ghana	– / –	2 / 0

Formed 1909 **Coach** Ivica Osim **Stadium** Arnold Schwarzenegger Stadion Graz Liebenau **Capacity** 15,400 **Address** Eggenbergergurtel 9, 8020 Graz **Website** www.sksturm.at

Sturm Graz

STURM Graz may not exactly be the terminators of the Champions League, but a club with the support of Arnold Schwarzenegger demands respect – especially since this is their second venture into the competition.

The Hollywood film star has a local family background and the club's stadium is named after him, but beyond that, Sturm are on their own as they take on the giants of the European club game.

At least veteran coach Ivica Osim insists that his players gained a great deal of valuable experience from last season's Champions League group stages when they tangled with Real Madrid, Internazionale and Moscow Spartak. Sturm – the name means "attack" – were founded in 1909, winning the Styria regional championship for the first time in 1921 and repeating the feat 11 times before the launch of a national league championship in 1950.

Only three of the initial 13 clubs came from beyond Vienna and Sturm found it difficult to compete for the best players.

Squad List

No.	Name	Date of birth	Position	Nationality	Domestic apps/goals	European Cup apps/goals
1	**Kazimierz SIDORCZUK**	04.03.1967	Goalkeeper	Poland	– / –	20 / 0
22	**Josef SCHICKLGRUBER**	21.07.1967	Goalkeeper	Austria	– / –	2 / 0
25	**Alexander KNEZEVIC**	14.10.1981	Goalkeeper	Austria	– / –	0 / 0
2	**Michael BOCHTLER**	15.10.1975	Defender	Germany	– / –	1 / 0
3	**Gunther NEUKIRCHNER**	02.12.1971	Defender	Austria	– / –	16 / 1
4	**Darko MILANIC**	18.12.1967	Defender	Slovenia	– / –	26 / 0
5	**Franco FODA**	23.04.1966	Defender	Germany	– / –	21 / 0
11	**Gyorgy KORSOS**	22.08.1976	Defender	Hungary	– / –	2 / 0
16	**Ferdinand FELDHOFER**	23.10.1979	Defender	Austria	– / –	0 / 0
24	**Ranko POPOVIC**	26.06.1967	Defender	Yugoslavia	– / –	13 / 1
27	**Georgios KUTSUPIAS**	11.02.1974	Defender	Greece	– / –	6 / 0
6	**Roman MAHLICH**	17.09.1971	Midfielder	Austria	- / –	17 / 2
8	**Markus SCHUPP**	07.01.1973	Midfielder	Germany	– / –	29 / 2
12	**Gilbert PRILASNIG**	01.04.1973	Midfielder	Austria	– / –	10 / 0
14	**Jan-Pieter MARTENS**	23.09.1974	Midfielder	Belgium	– / –	9 / 1
15	**Georg BARDEL**	08.03.1975	Midfielder	Austria	– / –	3 / 0
17	**Didier ANGIBEAUD**	08.10.1974	Midfielder	Cameroon	– / –	7 / 0
18	**Markus SCHOPP**	22.02.1974	Midfielder	Austria	– / –	15 / 0
20	**Mehrdad MINAVAND**	03.11.1975	Midfielder	Iran	– / –	2 / 0
21	**Tomislav 'Tomica' KOCIJAN**	21.11.1967	Midfielder	Austria	– / –	16 / 2
23	**Thomas GROBL**	19.12.1973	Midfielder	Austria	– / –	0 / 0
7	**Gerald STRAFNER**	03.06.1973	Forward	Austria	– / –	11 / 4
9	**Hannes REINMAYR**	23.08.1969	Forward	Austria	– / –	18 / 3
10	**Ivica VASTIC**	29.09.1969	Forward	Austria	– / –	19 / 8
19	**Imre SZABICS**	22.03.1981	Forward	Hungary	– / –	2 / 0
28	**Marko PANTELIC**	15.09.1978	Forward	Yugoslavia	– / –	0 / 0

Ivica Vastic: Sturm's principal source of attack.

They were relegated in 1954, promoted at their first attempt in 1955, but had to wait another 15 years before progressing into European competition in the 1970–71 Fairs Cup, where they fell to Arsenal in the second round.

Not until 1996 did Sturm finally see their name engraved on one of Austrian football's major prizes when they won the cup. Since that 3–1 win over Admira Vienna – six of their cup-winners survive in the Champions League squad – Sturm have proved virtually unstoppable at domestic level.

In 1997 they retained the cup by defeating Vienna 2–1 in the final. Then in 1998 they won the league championship for the first time in their history.

Sturm finished a staggering 19 points clear of second-placed Rapid Vienna. They scored 80 goals in their 36 league matches and boasted three of the five most successful marksmen in the championship – Mario Haas with 17 goals, Hannes Reinmayr with 15 and Ivica Vastic with 14. Unfortunately Sturm just missed out on the double, going down 3–1 to outsiders Ried in the cup final.

Sturm did at least gain revenge at the start of the following season – thrashing Ried 4–0 in the Supercup curtain-raiser to the season. Reinmayr scored twice.

The champions retained their crown this past season, but with nothing like the same ease as in 1998. The league title battle went right to the last day of the season before Sturm edged three points clear of Rapid. Then they crowned their season by winning the cup to claim their first-ever double. Not that Linzer ASK made it easy for them. The final ended in a 1–1 draw and Sturm won it only by virtue of a penalty shoot-out.

In the 1960s coach Osim was one of Europe's finest midfield generals for the Yugoslav national team, Zeljeznicar Sarajevo, Strasbourg, Sedan and Valenciennes. After retiring he bossed the Yugoslav national team and top clubs including Partizan Belgrade and Panathinaikos of Athens before settling in Graz in 1994.

No-one can doubt his ability to bring the best out of his players. Sturm may not have a squad replete with famous names, but they supplied five members of Austria's 1998 World Cup finals effort and their team spirit is renowned.

Sturm's attack was weakened during the summer by the departure of Haas for Strasbourg, but Vastic and Reinmayr remain to test opposing defences with their counter-attacking understanding. Experienced German veteran Franco Foda is the key man in defence, but Osim is under no illusions about the size of the challenge.

As he says: "We are a smallish club and every European tie is difficult, no matter who it is against. We are not a rich club, either, so we cannot afford the luxury of resting players for the big games. Not even Vastic, who is our main man – for example, if he does not score then we have problems."

Sturm Graz Records

European honours: None

Record European victory: 4–0 v Ujpest, Champions League qualifying round 1998–99

Record European defeat: 1–6 v Real Madrid, Champions League group phase 1998–99

Club records: Andi Pichler (410 matches), Gernot Jurtin (116 goals)

Record scorer in Europe: Ivica Vastic, 8

Record attendance: 15,400 (v GAK, March 15th, 1998)

Formed 1911 **Coach** Erik Brakstad **Stadium** Molde Stadion **Capacity** 11,000 **Address** Boks 316, 6401 Molde **Website** www.moldefk.no

Molde FK

MOLDE are fulfilling their destiny by appearing in the Champions League since the name bestowed on the club by their 32 founder members back on June 19, 1911 was ... International.

The Norwegian club are making their debut this season in the Champions League and are seeking to emulate the success of their fellow countrymen from Rosenborg Trondheim, who have run up a string of successes over some of Europe's finest.

Molde have unveiled a new stadium in time for the Champions League. Opened in April 1998, the Molde Stadion reflects the ambition of the club and the increasing success of Norwegian fooball at all levels. The average crowd over the past 18 months of 8,568 fans was an increase of around 5,000 over the steady attendance of previous seasons.

Only one element of stadium design took Molde by surprise when they gained access to the Champions League. That was the lighting standards demanded by the international broadcasters. At the last minute Molde had to borrow 25 high-power bulbs from the Ulleval national stadium in Oslo.

Managing director Jan Petter Storvedt said: "We couldn't find anyone else in the entire country who had such lights at such short notice. We'll keep these bulbs now and buy new ones for Ulleval!"

Molde was run as a traditional sports club until the early 1990s when they were transformed into a formal business venture as Molde Fotball AS, under the presidency of local man, Nils Olav Kringstad. While Molde may be considered a "small" club when compared with some of the other Champions League contestants, they boast 7,800 active members playing in 45 teams of varying standards and age groups.

Coach Erik Brakstad does not believe that the highly disciplined controls exerted over the players by top clubs in professional southern and western Europe are appropriate to Norwegian players. So, instead of shutting his players away in a secluded hotel or training camp before a big game, he is happy to let them relax at home.

That applies equally from new youngsters just out of the youth sections to the experienced stars such as Swedish defender Dennis Schiller – the only foreigner in the Molde squad – and Andreas Lund, the Norwegian league's leading scorer for much of this past season.

This is the first time Molde have competed in the Champions League, or even the Champions Cup, since the club have never win the Norwegian league and thus never had any previous qualifying permit. The air of unreality was exacerbated when they defeated first CSKA Moscow then Spain's Mallorca – last season's runners-up in the last Cup-winners' Cup – to reach the group stage.

Lund was the hero against Mallorca, his last-minute penalty sending Molde through on the away-goals rule.

Brakstad builds his tactics around a 4-3-3 model with an English-style flat back four controlled by Pal Lydersen, now happily settled back in Norwegian football after a short, unsettling spell in the English game with Arsenal. Behind them, in goal, is usually Morten Bakke, whom coach Brakstad considers one of the most-improved players in Norway.

Karl Oscar Fjortoft provides much of the dynamic energy which drives midfield, while most of his work, and that of his partners and the wingbacks is aimed at opening the way to goal for Lund and for teenage revelation Magne Hoseth – who was outstanding in the victory over CSKA Moscow.

Molde know, being realists, that the present opportunity offered by their presence in the Champions League may not be repeated for a long time. As Brakstad says: "We are a small club from a small nation. The way the Champions League is organised means that this, for us, is a unique opportunity to play against the best clubs in Europe.

"We have had to work hard to get here. It's a historic event."

Diplomatically modest, maybe, but then, what else might one expect from the coach of a club who number Prime Minister Kjell Magne Bondevik among their supporters?

Molde FK Records

European honours: None

Record European victory: 4–0 v CSKA Moscow, Champions League preliminary round 1999–2000

Record European defeat: 0–6 v Oster Vaxjo, UEFA Cup 1st round 1975–76

Club records: Stein Olav Hestad (680 matches), Jan Fuglset (164 goals)

Record scorer in Europe: Ole Gunnar Solskjaer, 3

Record attendance: 13,307 (v Rosenborg BK September 26th, 1998)

Karl Oskar Fjortoft: provides much of the side's dynamic energy from midfield.

Squad List

No.	Name	Date of birth	Position	Nationality	Domestic apps/goals	European Cup apps/goals
1	**Morten BAKKE**	16.12.1968	Goalkeeper	Norway	361 / –	12 / 0
12	**Are LERVIK**	10.10.1972	Goalkeeper	Norway	45 / –	1 / 0
13	**Knut D LILLEBAKK**	27.04.1978	Goalkeeper	Norway	1 / –	0 / 0
2	**Dennis SCHILLER**	18.05.1965	Defender	Sweden	59 / –	14 / 1
3	**Petter Chr. SINGSAAS**	23.08.1972	Defender	Norway	124 / –	7 / 0
4	**Pal LYDERSEN**	10.09.1965	Defender	Norway	74 / –	7 / 0
5	**Knut Anders FOSTERVOLD**	04.10.1971	Defender	Norway	241 / –	12 / 0
15	**Freddy DOS SANTOS**	02.10.1976	Defender	Norway	56 / –	6 / 0
17	**Trond STRANDE**	24.11.1970	Defender	Norway	243 / –	5 / 0
23	**Torgier Ramsli RUUD**	04.08.1979	Defender	Norway	1 / –	0 / 0
6	**Daniel Berg HESTAD**	30.07.1975	Midfielder	Norway	273 / –	12 / 1
7	**Jo TESSEM**	28.02.1972	Midfielder	Norway	71 / –	6 / 1
8	**Karl Oskar FJORTOFT**	26.07.1975	Midfielder	Norway	90 / –	10 / 1
10	**Odd Inge OLSEN**	28.12.1969	Midfielder	Norway	159 / –	8 / 0
16	**Magne HOSETH**	13.10.1980	Midfielder	Norway	13 / –	3 / 2
18	**Svein Tore BRANDSCHAUG**	11.05.1979	Midfielder	Norway	3 / –	0 / 0
25	**Glenn SAGDAHL**	04.01.1981	Midfielder	Norway	0 / –	0 / 0
9	**Andreas LUND**	07.05.1975	Forward	Norway	83 / –	6 / 1
10	**Ole Bjorn SUNDGOT**	21.03.1972	Forward	Norway	278 / –	9 / 0
11	**Andre Schej LINDBAEK**	01.11.1977	Forward	Norway	1 / –	0 / 0
14	**Thomas MORK**	22.06.1978	Forward	Norway	75 / –	6 / 0
19	**Anders HASSELGARD**	01.02.1978	Forward	Norway	66 / –	2 / 0
24	**Bernt HULSKER**	09.09.1977	Forward	Norway	2 / –	0 / 0
26	**Nils Gunnar THOMLE**	01.01.1981	Forward	Norway	0 / –	0 / 0
27	**Per Olav INDERHAUG**	04.01.1978	Forward	Norway	0 / –	0 / 0

Formed 1925 **Coach** Dusan Bajevic **Stadium** Spiros Louis
Capacity 74,767 **Address** Ipsilantou 170, 18535 Piraeus
Website www.olympiakos.gr

Olympiakos

OLYMPIAKOS are, quite simply, top dogs in Greece. Neighbours Panathinaikos are the only Greek club to have reached a European final, but their domestic achievements do not compare with the club from the Athens port of Piraeus.

Some 28 league titles and 21 cup wins set Olympiakos out in front of all the rest, including not only Panathinaikos, but popular outfits such as AEK Athens and PAOK Salonika. Their dominance since the introduction of full-time professionalism in 1979 has been emphatic – which is remarkable considering a number of controversies and ownership problems which have dogged the club simultaneously.

Yet they are still seeking to build a reputation beyond Greek borders, in European club competition. The best Olympiakos have so far attained is to have reached the quarter-finals in the Champions League last season when they very nearly beat Juventus. Olympiakos lost only 2–1 in the first leg in Turin and were 1–0 ahead – and thus leading on the away goals rule – until five minutes from the end of the return. Then midfielder Antonio Conte snatched a goal which edged Juventus, rather than Olympiakos, into the semi-finals.

Olympiakos, under coach Dusan Bajevic, did not enjoy the best of preparations for their new European campaign. Earth tremors which rattled Athens meant, naturally, that players, coaching staff and fans were distracted by more serious prior-

Squad List

No.	Name	Date of birth	Position	Nationality	Domestic apps/goals	European Cup apps/goals
1	**Kyriakos Nektarios TOHOUTOGLOU**	13.08.1972	Goalkeeper	Greece	136 / 0	9 / 0
22	**Kleopas GIANNOU**	04.05.1982	Goalkeeper	Greece	– / –	0 / 0
31	**Dimitrios ELEFTHEROPOULOS**	07.08.1976	Goalkeeper	Greece	79 / 0	12 / 0
3	**Kyriakos KARATAIDIS**	04.07.1965	Defender	Greece	352 / 3	45 / 0
5	**Georgios AMANTIDIS**	04.04.1970	Defender	Greece	173 / 7	20 / 2
6	**Elias POURSANIDIS**	13.04.1972	Defender	Greece	195 / 2	18 / 0
12	**Kofi AMPONSAH**	22.04.1978	Defender	Ghana	25 / 1	1 / 0
14	**Dimitrios MAVROGENIDIS**	23.12.1976	Defender	Greece	159 / 17	16 / 1
17	**Petros PASSALIS**	10.04.1974	Defender	Greece	156 / 4	18 / 0
19	**Athanasios KOSTOULAS**	24.03.1976	Defender	Greece	135 / 0	0 / 0
32	**Georgis ANATOLAKIS**	16.03.1974	Defender	Greece	173 / 5	20 / 1
35	**Paraskevas ANTZAS**	18.08.1976	Defender	Greece	65 / 5	2 / 0
4	**Andreas NINIADIS**	18.02.1971	Midfielder	Greece	128 / 25	13 / 3
7	**Stylianos GIANNAKOPOULOS**	12.07.1974	Midfielder	Greece	89 / 17	17 / 3
8	**LUCIANO De Souza**	21.08.1972	Midfielder	Brazil	102 / 29	6 / 1
11	**Pedrag DJORDJEVIC**	04.08.1972	Midfielder	Yugoslavia	123 / 30	19 / 4
18	**Vasilios KARAPIALIS**	13.06.1965	Midfielder	Greece	378 / 99	28 / 1
20	**Stylianos SFAKIANAKIS**	19.03.1976	Midfielder	Greece	48 / 7	1 / 0
25	**Zlatko ZAHOVIC**	01.02.1971	Midfielder	Slovenia	31 / 14	21 / 8
33	**Savvas POURSAITIDIS**	23.06.1976	Midfielder	Greece	74 / 14	0 / 0
2	**Konstantinos KARTEROULIOTIS**	10.12.1981	Forward	Greece	– / –	0 / 0
9	**Sinica GOGIC**	20.10.1963	Forward	Yugoslavia/Cyrpus	71 / 3	25 / 14
10	**GIOVANNI Silva de Oliveira**	04.02.1972	Forward	Brazil	129 / 48	21 / 10
24	**Peter OFORI QUAYE**	21.03.1980	Forward	Ghana	75 / 19	12 / 1
30	**Alexios ALEXANDRIS**	21.10.1968	Forward	Greece	287 / 228	34 / 4

Olympiakos Records

European honours: None

Record European victory: 5–0 v MPKC Mozyr, Champions League qualifying round 1997–98

Record European defeat: 0–5 v Gornik Zabrze, Cup-winners' Cup 1st round 1969–70

Club records: Giannis Gaitatzis (346 matches), George Sideris (224 goals)

Record scorer in Europe: Nikos Anastopoulos, 14

Record attendance: 73,537 (v AFC Ajax September 28th, 1983 and v SL Benfica October 19th, 1983)

ities than football. The entire opening round of matches in the Greek championship was also postponed which meant that Olympiakos launched their Champions League campaign with little more than four easy domestic cup ties and a few closed-doors friendly matches behind them.

One of those friendlies had a not-so-friendly outcome when Olympiakos were thrashed 6–1 by Fabio Capello's Italian club, Roma. Bajevic was furious at his players' lack of commitment and demanded that the board fine all of them £2,000 each. "As a performance by professional players, that was unacceptable," says Bajevic.

At least Bajevic believes that Olympiakos are significantly stronger, particularly in midfield and attack, than they were last season when they also met Real Madrid – opposition this time – in the group stages. The new men giving Bajevic cause for optimism were Brazilian international Giovanni from Barcelona – where he had fallen out with coach Louis Van Gaal – and Slovenia's Zlatko Zahovic from FC Porto – who thus faces his old club in the Champions League.

Giovanni cost Olympiakos a club record fee of £11 million and will be paying him £1 million-a-year. But if he can create or score the goals which take the club through to the knock-out stages of the Champions League and back to the top of the Greek league then it will prove to be money well spent.

Certainly it would delight the Andrianopoulos brothers who founded the club – complete with the title Olympiakos and the singular symbol of an athlete's head adorned with the triumphant laurel crown – in 1925. The brothers made up the club's original five-man forward line before going on to careers in local and national government which did the club no harm. Olympiakos rapidly developed into a sports organisation catering for all manner of leisure pursuits.

Football, of course, remained the prime sport and Olympiakos have almost always supplied the backbone for the national team. Star names down the years have included the likes of Nikos Anastopoulos, who was the best Greek forward and most-prolific marksman of modern times, as well as goalkeeper Nikos Sarganis and experienced defender Giannis Gounaris who was for years president of the Greek players' union.

As for coaches, however, Olympiakos' preference has been to look abroad. Outstanding managers have included one-time Yugoslav national manager, Todor Veselinovic, as well as Kazimierz Gorski, who led Poland to third place at the 1974 World Cup.

Now it is another Slav in Bajevic who, having been highly successful at neighbours AEK, has been charged with turning Olympiakos into international headliners.

Sinisa Gogic: leads the attack for the Greek champions.

Formed 1893 **Coach** Fernando Santos **Stadium** Estadio Das Antas **Capacity** 48,297 **Address** Estadio das Antas, Avenida Fernao de Magalhaes, 4300 Porto **Website** www.fcporto.pt

FC Porto

FC PORTO were, for years, considered merely the "third club" in the Portuguese football hierarchy until their thrilling Champions Cup victory over Bayern Munich in Vienna in 1987.

Events then and since have ensured that Porto, while their trophy count may not yet match that of Benfica, are considered the alternative centre of power in the domestic game. For one thing, they have now won more league championships than Sporting Lisbon (18 to 16), even if they still lag 12–9 in the cup glory stakes.

Their latest successes have depended on a comfortable mixture of home-grown Portuguese stars and imported talent. The latter have included, most notably, Yugoslav midfielder Ljubinko Drulovic and free-scoring spearhead Mario Jardel, who is just one of a string of Brazilians who have found a stylistic home from home in the northern Portuguese city.

Foreign players have long been central to Porto's successes and not merely when they beat Bayern in the 1987 Champions Cup Final thanks to the significant contributions of Polish goalkeeper Jozsef Mlynarczyk, Brazilians Celso and Juary and Algerian winger Rabah Madjer.

That was merely keeping faith with tradition since, way back in the early 1930s, Porto had been Portuguese pioneers in the international transfer market. They began by bringing in two Yugoslavs whose value was reflected in Porto's initial championship successes in 1938 and 1939.

In those days Porto's home was the old, rundown Campo da Constituciao. Now, as befits a club with European Cup-winning pedigree, their home is the impressive, Estadio das Antas with its 70,000 domestic capacity (reduced to 48,297 by UEFA security regulations for European ties).

Das Antas was chosen by Porto as the site for their new home in the early 1950s. It is situated in a north-eastern suburb of the city of Oporto and was inaugurated with a friendly match against Benfica on May 28, 1952. (Unfortunately Benfica spoiled the occasion by winning 8-2.)

Floodlights were added in the mid-1960s and capacity was expanded with an extra tier on the eastern side in 1976.

Yet the stadium remains only one, albeit major, feature in the expanding Porto "sports city". The surrounding complex also comprises a 7,000-capacity indoor arena, an indoor swimming pool and a large bingo hall.

None of this would have been possible without the income derived from the successes of the football team. Not

Mario Jardel: Porto is home from home for the Brazilian.

only have Porto collected prizes regularly at home but, in addition to the European Champions Cup, they also finished runners-up to Italian giants Juventus in the now-defunct European Cup-winners' Cup in 1984.

The creative force behind the club's progress in the 1980s was the late Jose Maria Pedroto. He took over in the mid-1970s and led Porto to the cup in 1977 and the league title in 1978 and 1979. After a brief spell under Austrian Hermann Stessl, Pedroto was recalled in January, 1982. Later his work was carried on by his pupil, former national team centre-forward Artur Jorge who coached Porto to their 1987 European title.

Porto further enhanced their image as members of the European establishment when they reached the semi-finals of the UEFA Champions League in 1993–94 under the guidance of Englishman Bobby Robson – whom Porto had snapped up after he had been ill-advisedly sacked in mid-season by Sporting.

Boss now is Portuguese coach Fernando Santos who was delighted when the club strengthened the team by bringing back national team goalkeeper Vitor Baia from Barcelona, where he had fallen out of favour with Dutch coach, Louis Van Gaal.

Santos says: "I like all my teams to play attacking football but that does not mean we play in a reckless manner. We know that against the best teams in Europe we will have to be patient and wait for our opportunities. A lack of patience has cost us dearly in the past in Europe but we must put that right because the Champions League is out main objective this season."

FC Porto Records

European honours: European Cup 1986–87

Record European victory: 9–0 v Rabat Ajax, European Cup 1st round 1986–87

Record European defeat: 1–6 v AEK Athens, European Cup 1st round 1978–79

Club records: Jaoa Pinto (407 matches), Fernando Gomes (288 goals)

Record scorer in Europe: Fernando Gomes, 17

Record attendance: 58,237

Squad List

No.	Name	Date of birth	Position	Nationality	Domestic apps/goals	European Cup apps/goals
1	**RUI Manuel da Silva CORREIA**	22.10.1967	Goalkeeper	Portugal	246 / 0	10 / 0
24	**Henrique HILARIO M. Alves Sampaio**	21.10.1975	Goalkeeper	Portugal	48 / 0	5 / 0
99	**VITOR Manuel Martins BAIA**	15.10.1969	Goalkeeper	Portugal	265 / 0	57 / 0
2	**JORGE Paulo COSTA Almeida**	14.10.1971	Defender	Portugal	184 / 13	31 / 2
3	**RUBENS Rodrigues Santos JUNIOR**	08.01.1975	Defender	Brazil	2 / 0	0 / 0
4	**ALOISIO Pires Alves**	16.08.1963	Defender	Brazil	282 / 13	48 / 2
5	**ARGEL Argelico Fucks**	04.09.1974	Defender	Brazil	1 / 0	0 / 0
7	**Carlos Alberto Oliveira SECRETARIO**	12.05.1970	Defender	Portugal	267 / 12	25 / 0
13	**RICARDO Alberto Silveira CARVALHO**	18.05.1978	Defender	Portugal	23 / 1	0 / 0
30	**'ESQUERDINHA'**	06.05.1972	Defender	Brazil	14 / 1	0 / 0
33	**RICARDO Emidio Ramalho SILVA**	26.09.1975	Defender	Portugal	51 / 2	0 / 0
45	**Antonio Leonel VILAR 'TONEL'**	13.04.1980	Defender	Portugal	– / –	0 / 0
6	**Emilio Manuel Delgado PEIXE**	16.01.1973	Midfielder	Portugal	146 / 4	14 / 0
8	**RUI Gil Soares de BARROS**	24.11.1965	Midfielder	Portugal	185 / 41	47 / 8
10	**RICARDO Andre Pinto de SOUSA**	11.01.1979	Midfielder	Portugal	16 / 5	0 / 0
14	**RODOLFO Luis Costa**	06.11.1976	Midfielder	Portugal	104 / 1	0 / 0
18	**Carlos Narciso CHAINHO**	10.07.1974	Midfielder	Portugal	136 / 7	2 / 0
20	**'PAULINHO SANTOS'**	21.11.1970	Midfielder	Portugal	162 / 6	40 / 0
29	**Anderson Luis de Souza 'DECO'**	25.08.1977	Midfielder	Brazil	19 / 2	0 / 0
9	**DOMINGOS Jose Paciencia Oliveira**	02.01.1969	Forward	Portugal	232 / 96	41 / 10
11	**Ljubinko DRULOVIC**	11.09.1968	Forward	Yugoslavia	214 / 48	32 / 7
15	**Miklos 'MIKI' FEHER**	20.07.1979	Forward	Hungary	6 / 0	1 / 0
16	**Mario JARDEL Almeida Ribeiro**	18.09.1973	Forward	Brazil	96 / 94	19 / 9
17	**ALESSANDRO Andrade de Oliveira**	27.05.1973	Forward	Brazil	3 / 0	0 / 0
21	**'CAPUCHO'**	21.02.1972	Forward	Portugal	248 / 38	26 / 0
26	**Carlos Eduardo Vertura DUDA**	15.03.1974	Forward	Brazil	8 / 1	0 / 0
27	**ROMEU Antonio Soares Almeida**	08.10.1974	Forward	Portugal	42 / 8	0 / 0

Formed 1902 **Coach** John Toshack **Stadium** Santiago Bernabeu **Capacity** 74,871 **Address** Concha Espina 1, 28036 Madrid **Website** www.realmadrid.com

Real Madrid

NO more regal a club exists in world football – never mind the European game – than Real Madrid, a record seven-times champions of Europe, twice champions of the world and a further record 27-times champions of Spain.

Add in two UEFA Cups and 17 Spanish cups and you have a record which has long since surpassed the ambitions of the students who founded the club as Madrid FC back in 1902. The Real title, meaning royal, was later granted by special permission of King Alfonso XIII.

Indeed Madrid's greatest teams have, down the years, performed in a regal manner – none more so than the side who won the Champions Cup for the first five years of its existence between 1956 and 1960. The 1960, 7–3 Champions Cup Final victory over West Germany's Eintracht Frankfurt is still revered by many as the greatest match ever played.

That, of course, has set an almost impossibly high standard for the successors of the likes of Alfredo Di Stefano, Ferenc Puskas and Francisco Gento in the famous all-white strip. Madrid teams have often appeared to freeze under the expectant pressure of fans steeped in their own glorious history.

The necessary answer is to spend heavily on the world's best players and no-one could accuse club president Lorenzo Sanz of holding back in the transfer market. A string of new stars were acquired to feed the insatiable appetite of the afi-

Squad List

No.	Name	Date of birth	Position	Nationality	Domestic apps/goals	European Cup apps/goals
1	**Bodo ILLGNER**	07.04.1967	Goalkeeper	Germany	88 / 0	38 / 0
13	**Albano BIZZARRI**	09.11.1977	Goalkeeper	Argentina	0 / 0	0 / 0
27	**IKER Casillas**	20.05.1981	Goalkeeper	Spain	1 / 0	0 / 0
2	**MICHEL Salgado**	22.10.1975	Defender	Spain	95 / 3	7 / 0
3	**ROBERTO CARLOS da Silva**	10.04.1973	Defender	Brazil	110 / 14	20 / 3
4	**Fernando Ruiz HIERRO**	23.03.1968	Defender	Spain	396 / 90	56 / 14
5	**Manuel SANCHIS Hontiyuelo**	23.05.1965	Defender	Spain	505 / 33	63 / 1
12	**IVAN CAMPO Ramos**	21.02.1974	Defender	Spain	91 / 5	5 / 0
17	**Javier DORADO**	17.12.1977	Defender	Spain	0 / 0	0 / 0
18	**Aitor KARANKA De La Hoz**	18.09.1973	Defender	Spain	140 / 2	10 / 0
21	**GEREMI Sorele Fotso Ndjitap**	20.12.1978	Defender	Cameroon	3 / 0	0 / 0
23	**JULIO CESAR Santos Correa**	05.04.1976	Defender	Brazil	63 / 4	3 / 0
6	**Fernando REDONDO**	06.06.1969	Midfielder	Argentina/Spain	241 / 12	30 / 1
8	**Steve McMANAMAN**	11.02.1972	Midfielder	England	3 / 2	30 / 5
10	**Clarence SEEDORF**	01.04.1976	Midfielder	Holland	110 / 15	36 / 3
14	**Jose Maria Gutierrez 'GUTI'**	31.10.1976	Midfielder	Spain	71 / 4	6 / 0
15	**Ivan HELGUERA**	28.03.1975	Midfielder	Spain	39 / 2	0 / 0
22	**Christian KAREMBEU**	03.12.1970	Midfielder	France	36 / 0	21 / 3
7	**RAUL Gonzalez Blanco**	27.06.1977	Forward	Spain	185 / 86	28 / 11
9	**Fernando MORIENTES Sanchez**	05.04.1976	Forward	Spain	157 / 65	32 / 6
11	**SAVIO Bortolini Pimentel**	09.01.1974	Forward	Brazil	49 / 10	8 / 3
16	**Samuel ETOO**	10.03.1981	Forward	Cameroon	1 / 0	0 / 0
19	**Nicholas ANELKA**	14.03.1979	Forward	France	3 / 0	9 / 1
20	**Elvir BALIC**	08.07.1974	Forward	Bosnia-Herzegovina	0 / 0	4 / 2

cionados – including Spain fullback Michel Salgado, England winger Steve McManaman and the controversial France striker Nicolas Anelka.

Their presence creates other pressures, particularly for Welsh coach John Toshack who – now in his second spell at Madrid – is charged with winning everything in sight both in Spain and in Europe.

Madrid might claim that a worldwide role was always the club's destiny, since they were not only among the founders of both cup and league competitions in Spain, but Carlos Padros, the Madrid president, attended the inaugural meeting of FIFA in Paris on Spain's behalf in 1904.

In the late 1920s Madrid launched a policy of buying big. They paid a then Spanish record fee of £2,000 for Ricardo Zamora, still revered as the greatest Spanish goalkeeper of all time.

The Spanish civil war in the late 1930s left Madrid's Chamartin stadium in ruins. The club had no money, but boasted one of the greatest visionaries in European football history. He was Santiago Bernabeu, a lawyer who had been, by turn, player, team manager, secretary and now club president. Bernabeu launched an audacious public appeal which raised the cash to build the wonderful stadium which now bears his name. The huge crowds which flocked in provided the cash to build the team which dominated the first five years of the European Champions Cup. Argentine-born centre-forward, Di Stefano, was the star of stars, scoring in all the first five Champions Cup Finals – an achievement which will, surely, never be equalled.

Bernabeu surrounded him with team-mates such as Hungary's Puskas, France's Ramond Kopa, Uruguay's Jose Santamaria and Brazil's Didi. Madrid won the Champions Cup again in 1966 and the UEFA Cup twice in the 1980s before regaining the Champions League in 1998. A single goal from Yugoslav striker Predrag Mijatovic was sufficient to earn victory over Juventus in the new ArenA stadium in Amsterdam.

Victory was achieved under German coach Jupp Heynckes who was succeeded within weeks by Guus Hiddink, who had coached Holland to fourth place at the 1998 World Cup finals. But even Hiddink could not satisfy the club's demands for success on every front. Within two months of guiding Madrid to victory in the World Club Cup in late 1998, Hiddink, too, had gone.

As even Mijatovic, the Champions League Cup-winner, once commented – echoing the complaints of other Madrid superstars such as Pirri, Santillana, Juanito, Hugo Sanchez and Emilio Butragueno – nothing they achieved ever seemed quite good enough. The 1960 team had been, if anything, too good.

Real Madrid Records

European honours: European Cup 1955–56, 1956–57, 1957–58, 1958–59, 1959–60, 1965–66, 1997–98; UEFA Cup 1984–85, 1985–86

Record European victory: 9–0 v B1913 Odense, European Cup 2nd round 1961–62

Record European defeat: 0–5 v Kaiserslautern, UEFA Cup quarter-final 1981–82

Club records: Manuel Sanchis (472 league matches), Alfredo Di Stefano (218 league goals)

Record scorer in Europe: Alfredo de Stefano, 49

Record attendance: 104,000 (v Atletico Madrid, June 14th, 1997)

Clarence Seedorf: one of a galaxy of international stars.

Formed 1900 **Coach** Ottmar Hitzfeld **Stadium** Olympiastadion **Capacity** 69,256 **Address** Postfach 90 04 51, 81504 Munich **Website** www.bayernmuenchen.de

Bayern Munich

BAYERN Munich are Germany's greatest modern football club with a great deal to prove after the dramatic manner in which last season ended amid both agony and ecstasy.

The record champions of Germany finished 15 points ahead of Bayer Leverkusen in the Bundesliga and had their hearts set on a historic treble. But first they lost the Champions League Final to Manchester United in those unforgettable two minutes of overtime, then they lost the German Cup Final to Werder Bremen after a penalty shoot-out.

"I have lost matches before like that – and won matches the same way," says coach Ottmar Hitzfeld, "but never at such a high level."

At least winning the German league title enabled Bayern to hold their heads up high as they return to the Champions League with a squad which has been strengthened during the summer. Not only by new players, either.

Bayern were handicapped towards the end of the last turn by the serious injuries which denied them the services of French World Cup-winning leftback, Bixente Lizarazu, and top-scoring Brazilian striker, Giovane Elber.

Now both are back to fitness after summer convalescence and fighting for their places in the spotlight alongside star newcomers such as veteran Swedish defender Patrick Andersson from Borussia Monchengladbach, Brazilian midfielder Paulo Sergio from Roma and Paraguayan teenage striker Roque Santa Cruz.

Bayern's experienced nucleus remains in goalkeeper Oliver Kahn, defender Markus Babbel, playmaker and skip-

Bayern Munich Records

European honours: European Cup 1973–74, 1974–75, 1975–76; Cup-winners' Cup 1966–67; UEFA Cup 1995–96

Record European victory: 10–0 v Anorthosis Famagusta, UEFA Cup 1st round 1983–84

Record European defeat: 2–6 v B1903 Copenhagen, UEFA Cup 2nd round 1991–92

Club records: Sepp Maier (473 Bundesliga matches), Gerd Muller (365 Bundesliga goals)

Record scorer in Europe: Gerd Muller, 67

Record attendance: 78,000 (2–0 v Real Madrid, April 14th, 1976 and 1–1 v Liverpool, April 22nd, 1981)

Jens Jeremies: the midfield dynamo is hoping to go one step further come May 2000.

per Stefan Effenberg, midfield dynamo Jens Jeremies plus the unique driving force provided by Lothar Matthaus – though he may be quitting Bayern in mid-season to wind down his career way out west with the New Jersey-New York MetroStars in Major League Soccer in the United States.

As coach Hitzfeld says: "Our plan to cope with the demands of the new Champions League, while maintaining our success rate at home, has been to have two top quality players for each position in the team. It will be of paramount importance to keep all our players fresh.

"We used a rotation system last season and we will do the same this season. You could see last May how injuries and fatigue played their part in our defeats in the Champions League and German Cup Finals. We do not intend to let anything like that happen again."

At least Bayern began the new season on a positive note when they defeated Bremen to win the curtain-raising league cup.

That was the 35th major prize for the Bayern trophy room: they have been Germany's champions on a record 15 occasions; have won the cup nine times; the league cup three times; the German Supercup three times; three European Champions Cups (in 1974, 1975 and 1976); the Cup-winners' Cup (in 1967) and the UEFA Cup (in 1996).

It is that history, plus the ongoing presence of former great players such as Franz Beckenbauer (now club president), Karl-Heinz Rummenigge (a director) and Gerd Muller (now a coaching assistant) which fuels the fans' optimism for a renewed duel with the likes of Manchester United.

Beckenbauer, of course, has been the pre-eminent personality in German football since he starred in midfield in the national team who finished runners-up at the 1966 World Cup in England.

He went on to win a then record 103 caps plus every prize possible before progressing first to coach with club and country (guiding Germany to World Cup success in 1990) and then as a politician (as president of Bayern and as a vice-president of the German FA with responsibility for the 2006 World Cup bid).

For all the on-pitch rivalry, no personal animosity exists between Hitzfeld and Manchester United boss, Sir Alex Ferguson, following United's extraordinary victory in Barcelona.

Hitzfeld says: "We have a good friendship. We talk together and phone each other. There is no problem between us because of what happened in Barcelona. That's sport and the game is finished after 90 minutes." Or 93 minutes in that case.

Squad List

No.	Name	Date of birth	Position	Nationality	Domestic apps/goals	European Cup apps/goals
1	**Oliver KAHN**	15.06.1969	Goalkeeper	Germany	280 / 0	51 / 0
12	**Sven SCHEUER 1**	9.01.1971	Goalkeeper	Germany	20 / 0	6 / 0
22	**Bernd DREHER**	02.11.1966	Goalkeeper	Germany	148 / 0	0 / 0
33	**Stefan WESSELS**	28.02.1979	Goalkeeper	Germany	0 / 0	0 / 0
2	**Markus BABBEL**	08.09.1972	Defender	Germany	219 / 10	40 / 6
3	**Bixente LIZARAZU**	09.12.1969	Defender	France	41 / 2	39 / 3
4	**Samuel Osei KUFFOUR**	03.09.1976	Defender	Ghana	63 / 2	19 / 1
5	**Patrik ANDERSSON**	18.08.1971	Defender	Sweden	176 / 10	18 / 1
10	**Lothar MATTHÄUS**	1.03.1961	Defender	Germany	452 / 120	90 / 17
25	**Thomas LINKE**	26.12.1969	Defender	Germany	206 / 15	32 / 2
30	**Nils-Eric JOHANSSON**	13.01.1980	Defender	Sweden	2 / 0	0 / 0
6	**Michael WIESINGER**	27.12.1972	Midfielder	Germany	53 / 3	0 / 0
7	**Mehmet SCHOLL**	16.10.1970	Midfielder	Germany	249 / 66	39 / 9
8	**Thomas STRUNZ 2**	5.04.1968	Midfielder	Germany	225 / 33	40 / 5
11	**Stefan EFFENBERG**	02.08.1968	Midfielder	Germany	289 / 60	34 / 12
13	**PAULO SÉRGIO S. do Nascimento**	02.06.1969	Midfielder	Brazil	124 / 47	19 / 8
14	**Mario BASLER**	18.12.1968	Midfielder	Germany	171 / 54	35 / 13
16	**Jens JEREMIES**	05.03.1974	Midfielder	Germany	122 / 4	15 / 0
17	**Thorsten FINK**	29.10.1967	Midfielder	Germany	279 / 37	25 / 4
18	**Michael TARNAT**	27.10.1969	Midfielder	Germany	194 / 15	25 / 1
31	**David JAROLIM**	17.05.1979	Midfielder	Czech Republic	1 / 0	0 / 0
32	**Emanuel BENTIL**	02.12.1978	Midfielder	Ghana	0 / 0	0 / 0
34	**Andrew SINKALA**	18.06.1979	Midfielder	Surinam	0 / 0	0 / 0
9	**Giovane de Souza ELBER**	23.07.1972	Forward	Brazil	140 / 65	21 / 8
19	**Carsten JANCKER**	28.08.1974	Forward	Germay	85 / 27	29 / 14
20	**Hasan SALIHAMIDZIC**	01.01.1977	Forward	Bosnia-Herzegovina	105 / 22	19 / 2
21	**Alexander ZICKLER**	28.02.1974	Forward	Germany	169 / 39	34 / 3
24	**Roque SANTA CRUZ**	16.08.1981	Forward	Paraguay	3 / 1	0 / 0

Formed 1913 **Coach** Eric Gerets **Stadium** Philips Stadion **Capacity** 30,024 **Address** Frederikloan 10 A, 5616 NH Eindhoven **Website** www.psv.nl

PSV Eindhoven

PSV have gained international kudos not so much as the sporting arm of the Phillips electrics corporation but through their own achievements.

They have won the Dutch championship 14 times – one fewer than Feyenoord, 13 fewer than Ajax Amsterdam – and the cup on eight occasions. On four occasions they were domestic cup runners-up while at international level they won the European Champions Cup in 1988 and the UEFA Cup in 1976. Along the way, PSV have also benefited from the services of some of the most outstanding Dutch footballers of the modern era, including Ruud Gullit and Ronald Koeman.

No wonder they believe their pedigree grants them status as one of the most dangerous of the outsiders in this season's UEFA Champions League.

In the 1960s Feyenoord took the international eye on behalf of Holland, an era which they climaxed by winning the Champions Cup and the World Club Cup in 1970. Then came Ajax Amsterdam's three-year domination of the Champions Cup – before PSV took their cue in style.

They won the UEFA Cup in 1978 with a team built around the intuitive attacking partnership of midfielder Willy Van der Kerkhof and his wing twin, Rene. Both were regulars in the Dutch national squad at the 1974 and 1978 World Cups, while combative defensive midfielders such as Jan Poortvliet and Ernie Brandts were also among Holland's World Cup stalwarts in Argentina.

It needed a 10-year gap and the development of a new generation of star players before PSV again made headlines in Europe.

In 1987–88 they were virtually irresistible at club level. Hans Van Breukelen was an outstanding personality in goal, Ivan Nielsen a Danish rock at the heart of defence, Jan Heintze a dangerous raiding leftback and Soren Lerby – another Dane – a feisty, energetic midfield dynamo.

Mix in the power-packed shooting of the young Ronald Koeman and the attacking talent of Wim Kieft and PSV presented a virtually unbeatable force.

It took a penalty shoot-out, however, for PSV to defeat the experienced old campaigners of Portugal's Benfica in the Champions Cup Final in Stuttgart. Koeman set the tone, after the game had finished 0–0 after extra time, by converting the first spot-kick. The next 10 were all scored as well until Van Breukelen finally stopped a shot by Benfica fullback Veloso and PSV had won 6–5 on spot-kicks.

Only a matter of weeks later, Van Breukelen, fullback Berry Van Aerle, midfielder Gerald Vanenburg and Koeman were completing an international double as members of the

Ruud van Nistelrooy: top scorer in last-season's Dutch league.

Squad List

No.	Name	Date of birth	Position	Nationality	Domestic apps/goals	European Cup apps/goals
1	**Ivica KRAJL**	26.03.1973	Goalkeeper	Yugoslavia	0 / 0	5 / 0
20	**Patrick LODEWIJKS**	21.02.1967	Goalkeeper	Holland	285 / 0	13 / 0
23	**Ronald WATERREUS**	25.08.1970	Goalkeeper	Holland	215 / 0	25 / 0
3	**Jürgen DIRKX**	15.08.1975	Defender	Holland	126 / 3	3 / 0
4	**Ernest FABER**	27.08.1971	Defender	Holland	176 / 6	23 / 0
5	**Jan HEINTZE**	17.08.1963	Defender	Denmark	317 / 6	41 / 0
16	**Chris VAN DER WEERDEN**	15.11.1972	Defender	Holland	115 / 7	17 / 0
21	**Yuri NIKIFOROV**	16.09.1970	Defender	Russia	28 / 1	36 / 9
25	**Stanislaus "Stan" VALCKX**	20.10.1963	Defender	Holland	317 / 23	34 / 0
30	**Andrei SKERLA**	29.04.1977	Defender	Lithuania	23 / 0	9 / 0
33	**Rob WIELAERT**	29.12.1978	Defender	Holland	2 / 0	0 / 0
35	**ABEL Luis da Silva Costa XAVIER**	30.11.1972	Defender	Portugal	19 / 2	23 / 1
6	**Mark VAN BOMMEL**	22.04.1977	Midfielder	Holland	144 / 14	1 / 0
7	**Dmitri KHOKHLOV**	22.12.1975	Midfielder	Russia	50 / 8	11 / 2
11	**Joonas KOLKKA**	28.09.1974	Midfielder	Finland	91 / 17	14 / 2
14	**Johann VOGEL**	08.03.1977	Midfielder	Switzerland	4 / 0	29 / 2
15	**Robert FUCHS**	15.02.1975	Midfielder	Holland	119 / 11	0 / 0
17	**Björn VAN DER DOELEN**	24.08.1976	Midfielder	Holland	55 / 2	10 / 0
18	**Eric ADDO**	12.11.1978	Midfielder	Ghana	0 / 0	15 / 0
19	**Dennis ROMMEDAHL**	22.07.1978	Midfielder	Denmark	56 / 7	13 / 2
24	**Ovidiu STINGA**	05.12.1972	Midfielder	Romania	37 / 6	12 / 0
34	**Igor DEMO**	18.09.1975	Midfielder	Slovakia	28 / 0	7 / 0
8	**Ruud VAN NISTELROOIJ**	01.07.1976	Forward	Holland	69 / 49	9 / 6
9	**Arnold BRUGGINK**	24.07.1977	Forward	Holland	152 / 51	9 / 3
10	**Luc NILIS**	25.05.1967	Forward	Belgium	140 / 93	70 / 34
22	**Wilfred BOUMA**	15.06.1978	Forward	Holland	75 / 11	2 / 0
28	**Tomasz "Tomek" IWAN**	12.06.1971	Forward	Poland	122 / 11	22 / 0

Dutch team who won the European Championship Final by 2–0 against the Soviet Union in Munich's Olympic stadium.

At one stage the Philips corporation allowed the sports club to exist almost as an autonomous entity. But as football grew ever more important as a promotional vehicle, so the company invested more money into both the impressive Philips stadium – with, naturally, its state of the art floodlighting system – and the coaching and playing staff.

One of the club's major coups was to sign up Bobby Robson to take over just as soon as he had led England to the semi-finals and fourth place in the 1990 World Cup.

Robson stayed two years, winning the championship both times, before moving on to Portugal with Sporting of Lisbon.

His star player was the Brazilian World Cup-winner Romario, who was duly succeeded by Ronaldo. In due course even Robson returned last year and it was a measure of his coaching ability that PSV – despite having sold half a dozen star names and suffering a prolonged injury crisis – managed to finish third in the table and reach the Champions League.

Belgian Eric Gerets took over as coach from Robson during the summer and was delighted to find PSV boasting one of the most lethal strike partnerships in Europe in experienced Belgian Luc Nilis and new Dutch talent Ruud Van Nistelrooy – who was the Dutch league's top marksman last term with a magnificent 31 of PSV's 87 goals.

That is a record to worry any opponent – however grand their reputation.

PSV Eindhoven Records

European honours: European Cup 1987–88; UEFA Cup 1977–78

Record European victory: 10–0 v Ards, Cup-winners' Cup 1st round 1974–75

Record European defeat: 1–6 v Saint Etienne, UEFA Cup 2nd round 1979–80

Club records: Willy Van der Kuylen (528 matches and 309 goals)

Record scorer in Europe: Willy van der Kuylen, 29

Record attendance: 30,024 (capacity repeated)

Formed 1873 **Coach** Dick Advocat **Stadium** Ibrox Stadium **Capacity** 50,467 **Address** Ibrox Stadium, 150 Edmiston Drive, Glasgow G51 2XD **Website** www.rangers.co.uk

Rangers

THERE is a big gap in Rangers' trophy cabinet. The Glasgow club have dominated Scottish football for a decade, but they've never won the European Cup.

Rangers brought the Cup-winners' Cup back to Ibrox in 1972. They were losing finalists in 1961 and 1967, but only twice – in nearly 40 years of trying – have they come close to the final of Europe's top competition. It still rankles at Ibrox that Rangers have never reached that exalted stage, while bitter rivals Celtic became the first British team to lift the trophy, in 1967.

In 1960, Rangers crashed 1–6 and 3–6 to Eintracht Frankfurt in the semi-final. In 1992–93, Graeme Souness's side – including Richard Gough, Ally McCoist and Alexei Mikhailichenko – pressed Olympique Marseille all the way in the final group phase of the Champions League. Rangers went through those six matches unbeaten. But Marseille grabbed a 2–2 draw at Ibrox; with hindsight, the crucial result in their passage to the final.

Since then, Rangers have under-achieved in Europe, despite the presence of stars like Paul Gascoigne and Brian Laudrup. One of their biggest problems has been the lack of competition in the Scottish League. Gone are the days when Celtic, Aberdeen and Dundee United could all take on Europe's best. Only Celtic, still a shadow of Jock Stein's team, can challenge the Ibrox club. Rangers' six-game winning start to the new season emphasizes their dominance.

Switching from the Scottish Premier to the demands of the Champions League was a task that taxed even a manager as shrewd as Walter Smith.

Now the ex-Holland coach, Dick Advocaat, leads Rangers into Europe. Among their opponents will be one of his previous clubs, PSV Eindhoven. Last season's runners-up Bayern Munchen and Valencia complete the group. He couldn't have asked for a much tougher draw.

"It's a very difficult section," says Advocaat: "But we have had to play very well even to reach this stage and we're looking forward to the challenge. Bayern will be favourites because they came within a couple of minutes of being European champions.

"But it's great for us and Scottish football that we're there. We worked hard and showed great character to qualify."

Rangers cruised past Finland's Haka Valkeakoski 4–1 and 3–0 to reach the third qualifying round. There, they pulled off a coup, to knock out UEFA Cup holders Parma.

Tony Vidmar and Claudio Reyna scored at Ibrox. In Italy, Rangers restricted Parma to Johan Walem's 66th minute goal. Scotland centre half, Colin Hendry, was immense, in a sophsticated defensive performance which suggests Advocaat is rebuilding Rangers' credibility in Europe.

Michael Mols: a Dutchman at home in Glasgow.

As midfielder Reyna said: "Parma were the toughest team we could have got. But we proved we were better."

The towering Hendry will be a key figure at the heart of Rangers defence, alongside the Italian pairing of Lorenzo

Amoruso and Sergio Porrini. The German Stefan Klos and the Frenchman Lionel Charbonnier contest the goalkeeper's place.

The Australians, Vidmar and Craig Moore can operate as full backs or wing backs, which gives Advocaat the option of switching between 3-5-2 and 4-4-2. He can also call on ex-PSV full back, Arthur Numan.

In midfield, Advocaat has options galore. He can ring the changes whenever he wants. Playmaker Reyna from New Jersey, the German Jorg Albertz, the Dutchman Giovanni van Bronckhorst, the energetic Pole Dariusz Adamczuk and the 21-year-old Scot, Barry Ferguson, are all competing for places.

If the coach wants an out-and-out winger, there's nippy Neil McCann, already a fixture in the Scotland squad.

Striker Michael Mols has begun the season with a batch of goals – seven in five league matches. Ex-Southampton and Leeds forward, Rod Wallace, is his likely partner. The Argentinian, Gabriel Amato, can cover for either. And if Advocaat needs to inject pace, he can send on Finnish international, Jonatan Johansson.

They may not be big-name stars, but Advocaat has assembled a squad with strength in depth. He is tactically astute; his man-management skills have brought the best out of players like Vidmar, Moore, Adamczuk and Wallace and there's a genuine spirit in the side. Says Reyna: "This is the closest team I've ever been with."

But do they have the quality to put Rangers' recent years of Champions League failure behind them? 'Gers fans hope that win over Parma gives the answer.

Rangers Records

European honours: Cup-winners' Cup 1971–72

Record European victory: 10–0 v Valletta, Cup-winners' Cup 1st round 1983–84

Record European defeat: 0–6 v Real Madrid, European Cup 1st round 1963–64

Club records: John Greig (858 games), Ally McCoist (355 goals)

Record scorer in Europe: Ally McCoist, 21

Record attendance: 118,567 (v Celtic, January 2nd, 1939)

Squad List

No.	Name	Date of birth	Position	Nationality	Domestic apps/goals	European Cup apps/goals
1	**Stefan KLOS**	16.08.1971	Goalkeeper	Germany	254 / 0	64 / 0
13	**Antti NIEMI**	31.05.1972	Goalkeeper	Finland	160 / 0	14 / 0
22	**Lionel CHARBONNIER**	25.10.1966	Goalkeeper	France	137 / 0	25 / 0
2	**Sergio PORRINI**	08.11.1968	Defender	Italy	248 / 10	58 / 4
3	**Craig MOORE**	12.12.1975	Defender	Australia	97 / 8	14 / 0
4	**Lorenzo AMORUSO**	28.06.1971	Defender	Italy	198 / 14	20 / 1
5	**Arthur NUMAN**	14.12.1969	Defender	Holland	329 / 39	37 / 3
14	**Tony VIDMAR**	04.07.1970	Defender	Australia	110 / 6	13 / 3
16	**Colin HENDRY**	07.12.1965	Defender	Scotland	459 / 41	13 / 0
17	**Dariusz ADAMCZUK**	21.10.1969	Defender	Poland	114 / 9	3 / 0
19	**Scott WILSON**	19.03.1977	Midfielder	Scotland	13 / 1	5 / 0
6	**Barry FERGUSON**	02.02.1978	Midfielder	Scotland	31 / 1	14 / 0
7	**Andrei KANCHELSKIS**	23.01.1969	Midfielder	Ukraine	265 / 62	16 / 2
8	**Giovanni VAN BRONCKHORST**	05.02.1975	Midfielder	Holland	150 / 31	34 / 4
11	**Jorg ALBERTZ**	29.01.1971	Midfielder	Germany	254 / 57	26 / 6
23	**Barry NICHOLSON**	24.08.1978	Midfielder	Scotland	6 / 0	1 / 0
26	**Ian FERGUSON**	15.03.1967	Midfielder	Scotland	319 / 36	39 / 3
27	**Derek McINNES**	05.07.1971	Midfielder	Scotland	268 / 20	7 / 1
9	**Michael MOLS**	17.12.1970	Forward	Holland	94 / 32	8 / 3
10	**Rodney WALLACE**	02.10.1969	Forward	England	374 / 116	14 / 4
12	**Claudio REYNA**	20.07.1973	Forward	USA	59 / 6	3 / 1
15	**Gabriel Omar AMATO**	22.10.1970	Forward	Argentina	173 / 40	7 / 3
18	**Neil McCANN**	11.08.1974	Forward	Scotland	171 / 28	8 / 1
20	**Jonathan JOHANSSON**	16.08.1975	Forward	Finland	31 / 8	12 / 7
21	**Marco NEGRI**	27.10.1970	Forward	Italy	89 / 34	6 / 3
24	**Gordon DURIE**	06.12.1965	Forward	Scotland	428 / 146	32 / 8
28	**Paul McKNIGHT**	08.02.1977	Forward	Northern Ireland	– / –	0 / 0

Formed 1919 **Coach** Hector Raul Cuper **Stadium** Mestalla **Capacity** 52,000 **Address** Antigua Senda de Sent 11, 46023 Valencia **Website** www.valenciacf.es

Valencia

VALENCIA must recover from a disastrous start to their Primera Liga campaign in time to steady themselves for the Champions League.

Many critics tipped Valencia to lead the domestic challenge to Barcelona. Indeed, Valencia won the Spanish Super Cup, beating Barca 4–3 on aggregate – 1–0 at Mestalla, 3–3 at Nou Camp. They also cruised past Hapoel Haifa of Israel to clinch a Champions League place. Now however, question marks have been raised against Valencia's back line, after Hector Cuper's side began the league season with three defeats against unfancied teams and conceded seven goals.

As midfield general Gaizka Mendieta saying: "We're excited about playing in the Champions League, but we're worried about not being at our best. Our bad start to the league season was a big blow to our morale."

On top of that Valencia, fourth in the Primera Division last season, knew they had been drawn in a tough opening group alongside Rangers, PSV Eindhoven and Bayern Munchen.

But Cuper has preferred to look on the positive side. "We want to make history in the tournament. That means we have to go on the way we did in the Super Cup and not think about our three defeats in the league."

Rangers striker Gabriel Amato played for fellow Argentinian Cuper at Mallorca. He is convinced Valencia won't be down for long. "They have some very good players and it's just a case of when they wake up," he said. "I just hope it won't be against us."

Claudio Lopez: the lure of Real Madrid was not strong enough for "The Bug".

Valencia's last European trophy came in 1980, when they beat Arsenal on penalties in the Cup-winners' Cup final. This will be their second appearance in the European Cup, and they have yet to reach the quarter-finals.

It's been "all change" at Mestalla during the summer. Last season, under Claudio Ranieri, Valencia enjoyed their best season since the early 1990s. Besides their strong league finish, they beat Barcelona in the Spanish cup final. Then Ranieri left for Atletico Madrid, and Valencia appointed Cuper, who'd taken Mallorca to the 1999 Cup-winners' Cup final on a shoestring.

Valencia were busy in the summer transfer market, but two of their best "signings" were already on the Mestalla staff. Skipper Mendieta turned down the chance to join Real Madrid, and agreed a new contract. So did the club's 1998–99 top scorer, Argentinian striker Claudio "The Bug" Lopez, who'd been interesting Real's bitter rivals Atletico.

Cuper is known as a defensive organiser, but Valenica spent heavily on attackers – maybe to play the counter-

Squad List

No.	Name	Date of birth	Position	Nationality	Domestic apps/goals	European Cup apps/goals
1	**Santiago CANIZARES Ruiz**	18.02.1969	Goalkeeper	Spain	156 / 0	0 / 0
13	**Jorge BARTUAL**	18.08.1971	Goalkeeper	Spain	9 / 0	0 / 0
26	**Andreas PALOP**	22.10.1973	Goalkeeper	Spain	35 / 0	0 / 0
2	**Mauricio PELLEGRINO**	05.10.1971	Defender	Italy/Argentina	1 / 0	0 / 0
3	**Joachim BJORKLUND**	15.03.1971	Defender	Sweden	26 / 1	31 / 0
4	**Francisco CAMARASA**	27.09.1967	Defender	Spain	267 / 7	11 / 0
5	**Miroslav DJUKIC**	19.02.1966	Defender	Yugoslavia	279 / 12	27 / 0
12	**Miguel Angel SORIA**	26.03.1974	Defender	Spain	0 / 0	2 / 0
15	**Armedeo CARBONI**	06.04.1965	Defender	Italy	66 / 0	35 / 2
16	**Alain ROCHE**	14.10.1967	Defender	France	31 / 0	54 / 3
20	**Jocelyn ANGLOMA**	07.08.1965	Defender	France	64 / 4	26 / 3
24	**Daniel FAGIANI**	22.01.1974	Defender	Argentina	2 / 0	2 / 0
28	**CARLOS Perez Villagrasa**	19.08.1979	Defender	Spain	0 / 0	0 / 0
30	**Manuel CABEZAS Garcia**	06.02.1978	Defender	Spain	0 / .0	0 / 0
6	**Gaizka MENDIETA**	17.03.1974	Midfielder	Spain	169 / 22	14 / 0
8	**Francisco Javier FARINOS**	29.03.1978	Midfielder	Spain	83 / 5	5 / 1
10	**Miguel Angel ANGULO**	23.06.1977	Midfielder	Spain	67 / 11	6 / 2
14	**GERARD Lopez Segu**	12.03.1979	Midfielder	Spain	42 / 7	2 / 0
18	**Christian Alberto "KILY" GONZALEZ**	04.08.1974	Midfielder	Argentina	93 / 15	1 / 0
21	**Luis MILLA**	12.03.1966	Midfielder	Spain	280 / 11	44 / 0
22	**Denis SERBAN**	05.01.1976	Midfielder	Romania	10 / 1	21 / 4
23	**David ALBELDA**	01.09.1977	Midfielder	Spain	42 / 2	2 / 0
7	**Claudio LOPEZ**	17.07.1974	Forward	Argentina	99 / 41	6 / 4
9	**OSCAR Garcia Junyent**	26.04.1973	Forward	Spain	100 / 23	10 / 3
11	**Adrian ILIE**	20.04.1974	Forward	Romania	44 / 22	16 / 17
17	**Juan SANCHEZ**	15.05.1972	Forward	Spain	162 / 39	10 / 5
19	**Goran VLAOVIC**	07.08.1972	Forward	Croatia	70 / 17	11 / 8

attacking game that Cuper favours. In came Spanish international forward Sanchez from Celta Vigo, promising midfielder Oscar from Barcelona, and the Argentinian midfielder Kily Gonzalez from Zaragoza.

On paper that gives Valencia a wealth of talent. Besides Mendieta and Lopez, they already boasted Romanian forwards Adrian Ilie and Denis Serban, the Croat Goran Vlaovic and pacy, skilful midfielder Miguel Angel Angulo, one of Spain's outstanding prospects.

"We have strength and we have cover," said Cuper. "Mendieta is a key player in midfield. Lopez is one of the most dangerous forwards in Europe. Sanchez, Oscar and Gonzalez should prove valuable additions.

"We'll need all our resources," added Cuper. "Because we're in one of the hardest groups of all. We're up against three athletic sides and we'll need to be at our best to qualify."

Which brings us back to Valencia's defence. Here they have looked unusually vulnerable for a Cuper side. The coach's success at Mallorca was built on a mean back four. That is what he must bring to his new club.

Valencia's two new Argentinian defenders, Daniel Fagiani and Mauricio Pellegrino, are still settling in. But Cuper declares: "We have a lot of good defenders. Miroslav Djukic, Joachim Bjorklund, Jocelyn Angloma and Amedeo Carboni immediately spring to mind.

"Last season, Valencia had a strong squad. Now I feel we're even stronger."

But Cuper will have to sort out that back line – and quickly – to prove it.

Valencia Records

European honours: Cup-winners' Cup 1979–80; Fairs Cup 1961–62, 1962–63

Record European victory: 5–0 v Hibernian, Fairs Cup quarter-final 1962–63

Record European defeat: 0–7 v Karlsruhe SC, UEFA Cup 2nd round 1993–94

Club records: Fernando Gomez (434 league matches), Edmundo Suarez "Mundo" (188 league goals)

Record scorer in Europe: Waldo, 32

Record attendance: 52,000 (capacity repeated)

Formed 1881 **Coach** Elie Baup **Stadium** Stade de Lescure **Capacity** 34,462 **Address** Rue Juliot-Curie, BP°33, 33186 Le Haillan Cedex **Website** www.fc-girondins-bordeaux.com

Bordeaux

BORDEAUX have a head start on all those worried coaches contemplating a packed fixture schedule as far as the footballing eye can see. They have been there, done it ... got the medals to prove it.

Lillian Leslandes: forms a potent attacking force with strike partner Sylvain Wiltord.

In 1995–96 this club from one of the world's great wine-growing regions began their competitive season on July 1 – and did not wind it up until the end of the following May. They played well over 60 matches in French league and cup, the InterToto and UEFA Cups. Bordeaux are proof that a positive and structured approach can bring massive rewards for those clubs who refuse to be intimidated by the prospect of a mountainous season.

What they achieved was a source of enormous pride for both the people of Bordeaux in particular and French football in general. They had not finished high enough to qualify for any of the mainstream European competitions so Bordeaux entered the summertime InterToto, qualified that way for the UEFA Cup and then went all the way to the final.

Never mind that they lost, ultimately, to Bayern Munich. Reaching the final was in itself a remarkable achievement from a team who boasted few players with any sort of international reputation.

That UEFA Cup run brought spies aplenty from foreign clubs. They liked what they saw in leftback Bixente Lizarazu, playmaker Zinedine Zidane and striker Christophe Dugarry. Equally impressed was national coach Aime Jacquet. Remarkable proof was beamed around the world two years later when Lizarazu, Zidane and Dugarry all starred in France's World Cup triumph over Brazil and the rest.

By then all three had moved away, but it says everything for Bordeaux's ability to attract players and the remarkable spirit bubbling within the club that they filled the gaps and won the French league championship for the fifth time last season after a nail-biting title race with old rivals Marseille.

Coach Elie Baup, who took over as coach from Guy Stephan early in 1998, deserves enormous praise for the manner in which he maintained his – and his squad's – cool under pressure while maintaining the attacking style which has earned them so many admirers. Not only that, but Baup held Bordeaux together despite a potentially morale-puncturing 6–0 thrashing by Parma in the UEFA Cup quarter-finals.

Baup tried, as best he could, to hold together last season's championship-winning squad. Ulrich Rame is a new hero of the fans in goal with Herve Alicarte the key man at the heart of a four-man defensive line. Jerome Bonnissel, a former captain of the French Olympic and under-21 team, is a raiding wingback with pace and skill while Stephane Ziani – who played alongside Bonnissel in Spain with La Coruna – is playmaker in midfield.

Up front Bordeaux are as dangerous as any French team with France striker Lilian Laslandes and league top scorer Sylvain Wiltord.

Former Bordeaux and France centre back Marius Tresor is among their greatest admirers. He says: "Bordeaux played some dream football last season and deserved to win the league. But the Champions League will be a difficult test. They are well organised and have a lot of skill and invention, but I'm not sure how some of the newer players will cope with playing in Europe."

Bordeaux are the second-oldest club in France, having been established as an all-sports club in 1881, with a football section created two years later. They won the French amateur championship in 1937 and turned professional two years later. They dominated wartime cup football in France and, five years after the end of hostilities, were league champions.

Dutchman Bertus de Harder – whose international career spanned 17 years from 1938 to 1955 – and top-scoring French international Edouard Kargu were heroes of that era.

Three times in the 1960s they were league runners-up and were then taken over by flamboyant Claude Bez in the 1980s. His reign brought Bordeaux three championships before he was ousted amid a financial scandal and subsequent relegation.

Just another reason why Bordeaux's presence in the Champions League should not be undervalued.

Bordeaux Records

European honours: None

Record European victory: 5–0 v Carl Zeiss Jena, UEFA Cup 1st round 1982–83, 5–0 v Bohemians Dublin, UEFA Cup 1st round 1993–94

Record European defeat: 0–6 v Parma, UEFA Cup quarter-final 1998–99

Club records: Alain Giresse (519 matches), Alain Giresse (158 goals)

Record scorer: Jean-Marc Ferreri, 8

Record attendance: 40,200 (v Juventus, April 24th, 1985)

Squad List

No.	Name	Date of birth	Position	Nationality	Domestic apps/goals	European Cup apps/goals
1	**Teddy RICHERT**	21.09.1974	Goalkeeper	France	57 / 0	0 / 0
16	**Ulrich RAME**	19.09.1972	Goalkeeper	France	63 / 0	10 / 0
30	**Francois DUBOURDEAU**	04.12.1980	Goalkeeper	France	0 / 0	0 / 0
2	**David JEMMALI**	13.12.1974	Defender	France	96 / 1	5 / 0
4	**Nisa SAVELJIC**	27.03.1970	Defender	France	52 / 1	14 / 1
5	**Jerome BONNISSEL**	11.04.1973	Defender	France	125 / 1	2 / 0
21	**Kodjo AFANOU**	21.11.1977	Defender	Togo	65 / 1	5 / 0
23	**Pascal PHILIPPE**	25.02.1976	Defender	France	1 / 0	0 / 0
24	**Herve ALICARTE**	07.10.1974	Defender	France	92 / 10	8 / 1
25	**Mathieu BEDA**	28.07.1981	Defender	France	0 / 0	0 / 0
6	**Jean-Christophe ROUVIERE**	04.08.1974	Midfielder	France	182 / 3	2 / 0
7	**Michel PAVON**	07.11.1968	Midfielder	France	351 / 40	9 / 0
8	**Johan MICOUD**	27.07.1973	Midfielder	France	201 / 38	13 / 4
10	**Stephane ZIANI**	09.12.1971	Midfielder	France	230 / 24	2 / 0
14	**Francois GRENET**	08.03.1975	Midfielder	France	114 / 4	19 / 0
15	**Corentin DA SILVA MARTINS**	1.07.1969	Midfielder	France	1 / 0	23 / 4
18	**Lassina DIABATE**	16.09.1974	Midfielder	Ivory Coast	54 / 2	10 / 1
19	**Marc ZANOTTI**	13.11.1975	Midfielder	France	1 / 0	0 / 0
20	**Laurent BATLLES**	23.09.1975	Midfielder	France	70 / 3	0 / 0
22	**Giuseppe COLUCCI**	24.08.1980	Midfielder	Italy	0 / 0	0 / 0
9	**Lilian LASLANDES**	04.09.1971	Forward	France	197 / 79	30 / 3
11	**Sylvian WILTORD**	10.05.1974	Forward	France	170 / 57	10 / 5
27	**Pascal FEINDOUNO**	27.02.1981	Forward	Republic of Guinea	7 / 1	0 / 0

Formed 1893 **Coach** Ivan Hasek **Stadium** Letna **Capacity** 21,362 **Address** Vladivostocka 1460/2, 100 00 Prague 10

Sparta Praha

EVERY step Dynamo Kiev took towards the Champions League semi-final last season twisted the knife into the hearts of the staff and supporters of Sparta Praha.

It was the final qualifying match. Sparta, at home at Letna, led 1–0 on aggregate through Miroslav Baranek's goal in Kiev. Two minutes were left. Then Andrii Shevchenko shot. Sparta defender Petr Gabriel ran back to cover as goalkeeper Tomas Postulka palmed the shot out. Instead, the ball hit Gabriel on the knee and flew past Postulka into the net.

Sparta – and thir fans – were demoralised. Extra time failed to produce a winner, but Yuri Dimitrulin's spot kick decided the penalty shoot-out in Kiev's favour.

Sparta captain Horst Siegl summed up: "Reaching the Champions League meant so much to the club, and our supporters. Now we must concentrate on our own championship and make sure we are in the Champions League in 1999–2000."

Sparta duly won the title again, despite a strong challenge from provincial club Teplice. With rare interruptions from city rivals Slavia, the Letna side have dominated Czech football since the 1989 "Velvet Revolution".

Martin Hasek: an experienced name in a developing side.

But Champions League football is crucial to Sparta. They are the most powerful club in the Czech Republic and attract the biggest crowds away from home. The problem is their own fans want to see them take on Europe's finest, not just cruise through Czech league matches.

For instance, only 5,784 watched them beat Viktoria Zizkov 2–1 at Letna in the Prague derby in August.

Sparta were drawn in a competitive group, with Spartak Moscow, Bordeaux and Willem II (Holland), but the feeling around Letna is that it's not as tough as the group they faced two years ago, when Sparta were drawn with holders Borussia Dortmund, Parma and Galatasaray.

Under the new Champions League rules, Sparta didn't have to qualify this time, but the question is, how have the Czech champions come through the upheavals of the summer? Previous sponsors East Slovak Steelworks – who also sponsored the Slovak club VSS Kosice – have gone, to be replaced by Labe-Vltava Press. That may be in Sparta's long-term interests, because Labe-Vltava are a vigorous media company backed by German capital.

Coach Zdenek Scasny has departed too. In his place is 36-year-old Ivan Hasek, the youngest coach in Sparta's history. His commitment to Sparta is undoubted. He won seven championships with them, three cups and was voted "Player of the Year" in 1987 and 1988. He finished his career with Strasbourg, then in Japan, but there was never any doubt that he'd return to Letna. He takes an upbeat position: "Playing in the Champions League is a great opportunity for the players and myself to prove that other clubs are not unbeatable."

Squad List

No.	Name	Date of birth	Position	Nationality	Domestic apps/goals	European Cup apps/goals
1	**Tomas POSTULKA**	02.02.1974	Goalkeeper	Czech Republic	107 / 7 1	2 / 0
22	**Michal CALOUN**	24.05.1970	Goalkeeper	Czech Republic	135 / 0	4 / 0
24	**Michal SPIT**	09.04.1975	Goalkeeper	Czech Republic	– / –	0 / 0
2	**Petr GABRIEL**	17.05.1973	Defender	Czech Republic	159 / 7	17 / 3
3	**Vladimir LABANT**	08.06.1974	Defender	Slovakia	49 / 1	11 / 2
5	**Michal HORNAK**	28.07.1970	Defender	Czech Republic	232 / 14	43 / 1
8	**Jiri NOVOTNY**	07.04.1970	Defender	Czech Republic	279 / 22	43 / 2
13	**Rene BOLF**	25.02.1974	Defender	Czech Republic	61 / 4	0 / 0
27	**Milan FUKAL**	16.05.1975	Defender	Czech Republic	75 / 7	6 / 2
4	**Martin HASEK**	11.10.1969	Midfielder	Czech Republic	173 / 18	11 / 0
6	**Zdenek SVOBODA**	20.05.1972	Midfielder	Czech Republic	188 / 25	27 / 2
7	**Jan FLACHBART**	03.03.1978	Midfielder	Czech Republic	– / –	0 / 0
12	**Vlastimil SVOBODA**	26.09.1972	Midfielder	Czech Republic	101 / 1	9 / 0
15	**Antonin MLEJNSKY**	17.05.1973	Midfielder	Czech Republic	– / –	3 / 0
17	**Pavel NOVOTNY**	14.09.1973	Midfielder	Czech Republic	146 / 24	25 / 1
18	**Petr PAPOUSEK**	07.05.1977	Midfielder	Czech Republic	– / –	0 / 0
21	**Michal SMARDA**	31.01.1971	Midfielder	Czech Republic	– / –	6 / 1
25	**Tomas ROSICKY**	04.10.1980	Midfielder	Czech Republic	– / –	0 / 0
9	**Vratislav LOKVENC**	27.09.1973	Forward	Czech Republic	193 / 60	26 / 7
10	**Horst SIEGL**	15.02.1969	Forward	Czech Republic	269 / 124	43 / 13
11	**Josef OBAJDIN**	07.11.1970	Forward	Czech Republic	153 / 39	14 / 12
14	**Libor SIONKO**	01.02.1977	Forward	Czech Republic	46 / 11	0 / 0
16	**Ludek STRACENY**	19.04.1977	Forward	Czech Republic	– / –	4 / 0
19	**Martin PROHASZKA**	18.08.1973	Forward	Slovakia	50 / 13	5 / 3
20	**Jiri JAROSIK**	27.10.1977	Forward	Czech Republic	49 / 2	2 / 0
23	**Miroslav BARANEK**	10.11.1973	Forward	Czech Republic	157 /38 1	2 / 3

Hasek names holders Manchester United, Barcelona and Bayern Munich as favourites, but he hopes Sparta can spring some surprises, like they did in 1991–92, the first season when the Champions League operated.

Sparta – including Siegl, Michal Hornak, Jiri Nemec, Martin Frydek and Hasek's current assistant Viteslav Lavicka – reached the semi-final group. They knocked out Rangers and Marseille to get there, then Kiev and Barcelona. Defeats in Barcelona and Kiev denied them further recognition, but that performance laid down a marker for the club's ambition – which Sparta haven't reached since.

This summer, Sparta had to sell two stars – Tomas Votava and Martin Cizek – to TSV Munich 1860, to fund Hasek's rebuilding programme.

Postulka, Hornak, Jiri Novotny, Baranek, Siegl and Vratislav Lokvenc remain pillars of the side. Hasek has brought in two players from Banik Ostrava, 25-year-old defender, Rene Bolf, and 22-year-old forward, Libor Sionko – who's already shown his worth as a sub for Siegl or Vratislav Lokvenc. Milan Fukal, another contender for the back three, arrived from Jablonec. Slovak international defender, Vladimir Labant, from Slavia, looks another shrewd buy.

Sparta have also made an important signing from Prague neighbours, newly promoted Bohemians – 21-year-old Jan Flachbart, probably the most technically gifted attacker of his age group. Slovak forward Martin Prohaszka adds strength to Sparta's back-up.

Hasek has been deliberate in his planning. "We have had to make allowances for the bigger format of the Champions League," he said. "Accordingly we have made several signings."

Their success may determine Hasek's future.

Sparta Praha Records

European honours: none

Record European victory: 10-0 v Anorthosis Famagusta, Cup Winners Cup 1st round 1964-65

Record European defeat: 0-6 v Leeds United, UEFA Cup 3rd round, 1970-71

Club records: Vaclav Masek (311 league matches), Oldrich Nejedly (170 league goals)

Record scorer in Europe: Ivan Mraz 14

Record attendance: 32,000 (v Slovan Bratislava, September 3rd, 1964)

Formed 1936 **Coach** Oleg Romantsev **Stadium** Central Dynamo Stadium **Capacity** 84,745 **Address** 1-st Koptelskiy per. 18/2, 129 010 Moscow **Website** www.spartak.com

Spartak Moscow

SPARTAK Moscow have won the Russian championship for six of the seven seasons since the collapse of the Soviet Union. But they want more – their ambition is to become the first Russian club to win the most prestigious prize of them all.

Spartak have scored some outstanding victories in Europe through the years – over the likes of Real Madrid, Ajax, Napoli and Arsenal, but they have never maintained the consistency which would take them through to a trophy presentation in front of a worldwide audience.

Now coach Oleg Romantsev, a former Spartak defender who has filled just about every administrative role at the club, believes he is pulling together a team of great talent. Romantsev has also worked hard behind the scenes to provide Spartak with the best opportunity to succeed – switching several league matches forward from autumn to spring so as to reduce the dangers of a fixture pile-up when the Champions League came around.

In goal is Alexander Filimonov, a former Russian youth and under-21 international who has made huge strides since joining Spartak three years ago from Tekstilshik Kamyshin. Dmitri Khlestov and Yuri Kovtun are experienced international defenders, while in midfield and attack the creative inspiration comes from Andrei Tikhonov and Ilia Tsimbalar. These are two of Russian football's most-experienced campaigners at international club level with around 50 matches each to their credit.

Squad List

No.	Name	Date of birth	Position	Nationality	Domestic apps/goals	European Cup apps/goals
1	**Alexandr FILIMONOV**	15.10.1973	Goalkeeper	Russia	– / –	31 / 0
12	**Sergei KOTOV**	17.03.1982	Goalkeeper	Russia	– / –	0 / 0
22	**Andrei SMETANIN**	21.06.1969	Goalkeeper	Russia	– / –	19 / 0
2	**Yuri KOVTUN**	05.01.1970	Defender	Russia	– / –	17 / 0
3	**Dmitri KHLESTOV**	21.01.1971	Defender	Russia	– / –	47 / 2
5	**Evgeni BOUSCHMANOV**	02.11.1971	Defender	Russia	– / –	27 / 2
6	**Dmitri ANANKO**	29.09.1973	Defender	Russia	– / –	37 / 0
14	**Vadim EVSEEV**	08.01.1976	Defender	Russia	– / –	16 / 1
15	**Miroslav ROMASCHENKO**	16.12.1973	Defender	Belarus	– / –	12 / 1
17	**Eduard MOR**	04.10.1977	Defender	Russia	– / –	0 / 0
18	**Dmitri PARFIONOV**	11.09.1974	Defender	Ukraine	– / –	27 / 0
7	**Vassili BARANOV**	05.10.1972	Midfielder	Russia	– / –	9 / 0
8	**Victor BULATOV**	22.01.1972	Midfielder	Russia	– / –	2 / 0
10	**Valeri KETCHINOV**	05.08.1974	Midfielder	Russia	– / –	27 / 4
11	**Andrei TIKHONOV**	16.10.1970	Midfielder	Russia	– / –	44 / 16
13	**EVERTON Peniche**	16.01.1979	Midfielder	Brazil	– / –	0 / 0
16	**Alexei MELESCHIN**	30.01.1976	Midfielder	Russia	– / –	12 / 2
19	**Alexei ZLIDNEV**	23.05.1980	Midfielder	Russia	– / –	0 / 0
4	**Ilia TSIMBALAR**	17.06.1969	Forward	Russia	– / –	47 / 11
9	**Egor TITOV**	29.05.1976	Forward	Russia	– / –	28 / 7
20	**Alexandr SCHIRKO**	24.11.1976	Forward	Russia	– / –	22 / 9
21	**Artem BEZRODNYI**	10.02.1979	Forward	Russia	– / –	6 / 0
24	**Luis ROBSON Pereira Silva 2**	1.09.1974	Forward	Brazil	– / –	16 / 2
25	**Anatoli KANISCHEV**	11.12.1971	Forward	Russia	– / –	14 / 0

Tikhonov is a Spartak youth product and a former Soviet youth international who was both Spartak's 16-goal top scorer and voted Footballer of the Year in 1996. It was a major surprise – which the federation may still regret – that Tikhonov was omitted from the national squad which reached the finals of the Euroepean Championship that year.

Tsimbalar, now 30 and slower after a series of serious injuries, remains one of the most intelligent of Russian playmakers – with great vision and a delicate touch whether passing the ball long or short.

Ukraine-born Tsimbalar joined Spartak from Chernomorets Odessa in 1992. It was a subject of some controversy when, after the collapse of the Soviet Union, he chose to continue his national team career with Russia rather than his native Ukraine.

Tikhonov and Tsimbalar are just the latest members of an exclusive club of outstanding players to have served Spartak down the years – and established a tradition and pride which always makes them dangerous opponents. Such Soviet heroes of the "old" days included the likes of 1950s' top scorer, Nikita Simonian, and lefthalf Igor Netto, who starred in the Soviet side who won Olympic gold in Melbourne in 1956.

For years the club was ruled by the most respected members of the managerial old guard in veteran president, Nikolai Starostin, and former national coach, Constantin Beskov, who handed over the managerial reins, in due course, to his favoured pupil Romantsev.

Under Romantsev – who has also doubled as national team manager – Spartak bridged the political upheavals of the early 1990s and maintained their command of the domestic championship. They achieved all that despite having proved unable to hold onto star players such as Vasili Kulkov, Igor Shalimov, Alexander Mostovoi, Viktor Onopko and Mikhail Beschastnikh.

Spartak regularly make the headlines. In November 1996 they won the Russian championship in a play-off, beating Spartak Vladikavkaz 2–1 in St Petersburg with goals from Tsimbalar and Tikhonov. The two teams had each ended the season with 72 points each though Spartak did have the better goal difference.

Spartak Moscow Records

European honours: None

Record European victory: 5–0 v Jeunesse Esch, European Cup 1st round 1980–81; 5-0 v HJK Helsinki, UEFA Cup 1st round 1983–84; 5–0 v Skonto Riga, European Cup 1st round 1993–94; 5–0 v Litex Lovech, Champions League qualifying round 1998–99

Record European defeat: 1–6 v Werder Bremen, UEFA Cup 2nd round 1987–88

Club records: Feodor Cherenkov (398 matches), Nikita Simonjan (135 goals)

Record scorer in Europe: Sergei Rodionov, 22

Record attendance: 103,000 (former international record)

Spartak remain the most affluent club in Russian football, but that has not spared them from having to cope with a crisis in the domestic game which brought a general slump in attendances, the emergence of a hooligan tendency among supporters and a lowering of morale caused by the national team's failure to qualify for the 1998 World Cup finals.

All the more important then, that Spartak do well in the Champions League.

Andrei Tikhonov: Russia's Footballer of the Year in 1996.

Formed 1896 **Coach** Co Adriaanse **Stadium** Willem II Stadion
Capacity 14,700 **Address** Postbus 235, 5000 AE Tilburg
Website www. willem-ii.nl

Willem II

WILLEM II stand out in any football company because of their unusual name which they owe to King William II who ruled the kingdom of Holland-Flanders from the town of Tilburg almost 200 years ago.

Any of Willem II's players who thought that Adriaanse would bring a gentle, sensitive manner with him after years of working with youngsters, were in for a shock. Adriaanse knows exactly what he wants from his players, in terms of discipline, style, technique and tactics. Willem II had nearly been relegated weeks before Adriaanse took over in 1997 and he warned anyone who cared to listen that full-grown, well-paid professionals would be expected to reach much higher standards than schoolboy apprentices.

His approach did not go down well initially, but results since speak for themselves. Adrianse, who had previously been senior coach with PEC Zwolle and Den Haag, has brought Willem II back towards the proud status they once held in the Dutch game – but that was back in the amateur era.

Founded in 1896, Willem II have won the championship three times, in 1916, 1952 and 1955. They have won the cup twice, but those victories are a long way back as well, in 1944 and 1963. Their European pedigree is also a modest one. They first stepped up onto the international stage in the 1963–64 Cup-winners' Cup and were thrashed 7–2 on aggre-

Squad List

No.	Name	Date of birth	Position	Nationality	Domestic apps/goals	European Cup apps/goals
1	**Kris MAMPAEY**	02.11.1970	Goalkeeper	Belgium	25 / 0	2 / 0
16	**Jim van FESSEM**	07.08.1975	Goalkeeper	Holland	107 / 0	4 / 0
24	**Casper NELIS**	12.06.1976	Goalkeeper	Holland	0 / 0	0 / 0
2	**Geoffrey PROMMAYON**	25.10.1971	Defender	Thailand/Holland	151 / 0	8 / 0
3	**Delano HILL**	29.04.1975	Defender	Holland	79 / 4	4 / 0
4	**Marco GENTILE**	25.05.1968	Defender	Holland	97 / 4	0 / 0
5	**Raymond VICTORIA**	10.10.1972	Defender	Holland	106 / 10	0 / 0
15	**Mark SCHENNING**	18.10.1970	Defender	Holland	188 / 15	4 / 1
17	**Reinder HENDRIKS**	26.04.1973	Defender	Holland	107 / 4	1 / 0
21	**Jos van NIEUWSTADT**	19.11.1979	Defender	Holland	1 / 0	0 / 0
22	**Joris MATHIJSEN**	05.04.1980	Defender	Holland	1 / 0	0 / 0
22	**Guy VELDMAN**	14.12.1978	Defender	Belgium	0 / 0	0 / 0
25	**Kew JALIENS**	15.09.1978	Defender	Holland	68 / 3	0 / 0
6	**Marcel VALK**	18.04.1967	Midfielder	Holland	229 / 30	4 / 1
8	**Arno ARTS**	26.06.1969	Midfielder	Holland	222 / 37	6 / 1
10	**Tomas GALASEK**	15.01.1973	Midfielder	Czech Republic	83 / 8	6 / 0
12	**Dmitri SHOUKOV**	29.09.1975	Midfielder	Russia	81 / 12	5 / 0
13	**Danny LANDZAAT**	06.05.1976	Midfielder	Holland	73 / 8	1 / 0
14	**Adil RAMZI**	14.07.1977	Midfielder	Moroccan	35 / 12	4 / 2
7	**Jatto CEESAY**	16.11.1974	Forward	Gambia	94 / 14	4 / 1
9	**Mariano BOMBARDA**	10.09.1972	Forward	Argentina/Italy	143 / 66	4 / 1
11	**Yassine ABDELLAOUI**	21.06.1975	Forward	Morocco	152 / 19	4 / 0
18	**Dennis SCHULP**	18.01.1978	Forward	Holland	51 / 12	1 / 0
19	**Ousmane SANOU**	11.03.1978	Forward	Burkina Faso	52 / 9	- / -
20	**Erwin HERMES**	16.12.1969	Forward	Holland	24 / 0	0 / 0

gate by Manchester United – led by Bobby Charlton and Denis Law who scored a second-leg hat-trick.

Until last season's UEFA Cup, Willem II had never beyond the first round in Europe. They made history by defeating Dynamo Tbilisi, former winners of the Cup-winners' Cup, 3–0 and 3–0, but then they fell to Spain's Betis of Seville. Only a late goal by Mariano Bombarda allowed Willem II to snatch a 1–1 draw at home before losing the return 3–0.

That disappointment was quickly forgotten in the excitement over Willem II's finest league campaign for years. In the end they finished 15 points behind champions Feyenoord, but that was still good enough for second place and entry, for the first time, into the Champions League.

The challenge for Adriaanse in preparing for the Champions Cup was in rebuilding the nucleus of his defence after the summer departure of Finland international Sami Hyppia to Liverpool. Willem II brought in several new defenders including one, Marco Gentile, with a surname which should strike fear into the hearts of opponents with memories stretching back to World Cups and other top tournaments in the 1980s.

Whether Marco is quite up to the ruthlessly effective defensive standards of the old Juventus stalwart, Claudio Gentile, is another matter. This is a sector of the team in which Willem II may suffer ongoing problems before Adriaanse is happy with his solutions.

At least in midield and attack Willem II are well directed and organised, courtesy of the vision and skill of Czech playmaker Tomas Galasek. Arno Arts and Adil Ramzy – scorer of two goals against Tbilisi last season – provide midfield support and Argentine forward Bombarda may surprise opposition defences with his pace and enthusiasm.

Adriaanse considers Galasek to be Willem II's most important player in the Champions League, since the club's success will depend more on the efficiency of their attack than their defence. After all, it was thanks to their element of attacking surprise that Willem II secured a remarkable 34 points in their final 13 league games last term to rise from midtable to runners-up.

"We will not be making any special plans for the Champions League compared with our normal games," says Adriaanse. "After all, it's only six games in the first stage of the group section, so by the time you have adapted it's all over ... and you are either in or out."

Adil Ramzi: the Moroccan who is part of a well-directed midfield.

Willem II Records

European honours: None

Record European victory: 3–0 v Dynamo Tbilisi, UEFA Cup 1st round 1998–99

Record European defeat: 0–6 v Manchester United, Cup-winners' Cup 1st round 1963–64

Club records: John Feskens (483 matches), Piet de Jong (216 goals)

Record scorer in Europe: Adil Ramzi, 2

Record attendance: 23,000 (v Botafogo, May 1968)

Formed 1905 **Coach** Gianluca Vialli **Stadium** Stamford Bridge **Capacity** 35,461 **Address** Stamford Bridge, London SW6 1HS **Website** www.chelseafc.co.uk

Chelsea

CHELSEA have had to wait a long time to take part in Europe's top club competition. League champions in 1955, they were due to be England's first representatives in the European Cup. Instead – under pressure from the Football League – they stayed out. It was 44 years until the Blues got another chance.

Third in the Premiership last season, Chelsea beat Skonto Riga 3–0 at Stamford Bridge, then drew 0–0 in Latvia, to reach the Champions League via the third qualifying round.

Chelsea, one of London's top three clubs, have come a long way in a short time. Chairman Ken Bates remembers the trials of an earlier decade, when the Blues yo-yoed between divisions – "The Champions League seems light years away from the days when we were playing the likes of Tranmere, Reading, Swindon and Barnsley."

Since 1995 – when they lost the Cup-winners' Cup semi-final to Zaragoza – Chelsea have invested massively in foreign stars. Ruud Gullit was the first. Now the Blues boast the most polyglot team in a polyglot Premiership.

Typically, they're managed by one of Italy's great post-war forwards, Gianluca Vialli. Sometimes there are only one or two Englishmen in the starting line-up.

That does not bother Chelsea fans, who are looking forward to the greatest era in the club's history. The Blues won the Cup-winners' Cup in 1971 and 1998 – the latter triumph over Stuttgart was another landmark in the development of the "new" Chelsea. With a wealth of experience in the side, they look well equipped to compete in the Champions League.

Vialli said: "There are a lot of games to be played, but I don't think we'll feel tired, because there's such a great atmosphere about the Champions League. I have a big squad with a lot of quality players which gives me confidence. I'm not concerned about the draw. If we're going to go far in the competition, we have to beat the best in Europe."

Ex-Milan star Marcel Desailly and summer signing Didier Deschamps have done that already. Centre back Desailly gained winner's medals with both Marseille and Milan.

Chelsea Records

European honours: Cup-winners' Cup 1970–71, 1997–98

Record European victory: 13–0 v Jeunesse Hautcharage, Cup-winners' Cup 1st round 1971–72

Record European defeat: 0–5 v Barcelona, UEFA Cup semi-final 1965–66

Club records: Ron Harris (795 games), Bobby Tambling (202 goals)

Record scorer in Europe: Peter Osgood, 16

Record attendance: 82,905 (v Arsenal, October 12th, 1935)

Gianfranco Zola: keen to perform on the top stage.

Squad List

No.	Name	Date of birth	Position	Nationality	Domestic apps/goals	European Cup apps/goals
1	**Ed DE GOEY**	20.12.1966	Goalkeeper	Holland	68 / 0	57 / 0
13	**Kevin HITCHCOCK**	05.10.1962	Goalkeeper	England	295 / 0	4 / 0
23	**Carlo CUDICINI**	06.09.1973	Goalkeeper	Italy	0 / 0	3 / 0
2	**Dan Vasile PETRESCU**	22.12.1967	Defender	Romania	163 / 18	29 / 4
3	**Celestine BABAYARO**	29.08.1978	Defender	Nigeria	41 / 3	23 / 2
4	**Jes HOGH**	07.05.1966	Defender	Denmark	1 / 0	29 / 2
5	**Frank LEBOEUF**	22.01.1968	Defender	France	96 / 15	22 / 3
6	**Marcel DESAILLY**	07.09.1968	Defender	France	35 / 0	52 / 4
14	**Graeme LE SAUX**	17.10.1968	Defender	England	279 / 17	18 / 0
15	**Mario MELCHIOT**	04.11.1976	Defender	Holland	0 / 0	13 / 1
17	**Albert FERRER**	06.06.1970	Defender	Spain	35 / 0	64 / 1
21	**Bernard LAMBOURDE**	11.05.1971	Defender	France	24 / 0	6 / 1
26	**John TERRY**	07.12.1980	Defender	England	2 / 0	1 / 0
33	**Luca PERCASI**	25.08.1980	Defender	Italy	0 / 0	0 / 0
7	**Didier DESCHAMPS**	15.10.1968	Midfielder	France	2 / 0	65 / 0
8	**Gustavo POYET**	15.11.1967	Midfielder	Uruguay	47 / 17	31 / 10
11	**Dennis WISE**	16.12.1966	Midfielder	England	406 / 76	24 / 2
12	**Bjarne GOLDBAEK**	06.10.1968	Midfielder	Denmark	26 / 5	21 / 4
16	**Roberto DI MATTEO 2**	9.05.1970	Midfielder	Italy	95 / 13	30 / 3
18	**Gabriele AMBROSETTI**	07.08.1973	Midfielder	Italy	2 / 0	7 / 2
20	**Jody MORRIS**	22.12.1978	Midfielder	England	46 / 2	4 / 0
24	**Samuele DALLA BONA**	06.02.1981	Midfielder	Italy	0 / 0	0 / 0
9	**Chris SUTTON**	10.03.1973	Forward	England	5 / 0	16 / 2
10	**Tore Andre FLO**	15.06.1973	Forward	Norway	69 / 22	28 / 6
22	**Mark NICHOLLS**	30.05.1977	Forward	England	36 / 3	5 / 0
25	**Gianfranco ZOLA**	05.07.1966	Forward	Italy	92 / 30	54 / 13
32	**Mikael FORSSELL**	15.03.1981	Forward	Finland	10 / 1	5 / 0

Deschamps won the trophy with Marseille and Juventus.

Both played for France's 1998 World Cup winners. So did centre back Frank Leboeuf.

Deschamps adds solidity and makes an effective "shield" for the back four. Desailly is "one of the world's top six centre backs", according to Vialli. "He has great presence. We need strong people on the pitch and Marcel is one of them."

Both will be key figures in Chelsea's campign. So, too, will Gianfranco Zola. The little Sardinian attacker says he still has "things to prove".

"We have played against some good sides in the Cup-winners' Cup. But now it's different. We're up against some of the best teams in Europe. We're learning all the time, myself and the team as a whole. That's good for me, because the day I don't feel I have things to prove will be the day that I stop playing."

Milan have already targeted him as the fulcrum of Chelsea's attack. Coach Alberto Zaccheroni has also warned his side about the aerial threat posed by Tore Andre Flo, Gustavo Poyet and Chris Sutton. But Milan also noted the number of players over 30 – like Desailly, Deschamps and Zola for starters – in the Blues' squad.

Wherever you look though, Chelsea have strength in depth. In goal, ex-Feyenoord man Ed De Goey is understudied by ex-Milan keeper Carlo Cudicini.

Desailly and Leboeuf are the resident central defenders. That partnership was so frustrating for promising English centre back Michael Duberry that he joined Leeds in the summer. Ex-Ajax centre back Mario Melchiot and Danish international Jes Hogh provide cover. At full back, Vialli can pick from Albert Ferrer, a European Cup winner with Barcelona in 1992, the Nigerian Celestine Babayaro and England left back Graeme Le Saux.

Ex-Vicenza winger Gabriele Ambrosetti supplies midfield width. So does the Romanian international Dan Petrescu. Both are expected to deliver quality crosses to Chelsea's big men.

Poyet is one of the Premiership's most prolific strikers from midfield. Roberto Di Matteo scored the fastest goal ever in an F.A. Cup Final. Alongside Deschamps, skipper Dennis Wise shows the energy of a worker ant. He needs to watch himself though – he's collected too many cards over the years.

That leaves Zola up front, with either Flo or Sutton, a £10 million summer signing from Blackburn. Sutton has bad memories of Rovers' disastrous 1995–96 Champions League campaign. Now he's hoping for glory with Chelsea.

As long as Vialli's batch of 30-somethings keep going, the Blues can chase that dream.

Formed 1905 **Coach** Fatih Terim **Stadium** Ali Sami Yen Stadi
Capacity 24,000 **Address** Metin Oktay Tesisleri, Florya, Istanbul
Website www.galatasaray.org.tr

Galatasaray

WHEN Galatasaray and arch rivals Fenerbahce drew in the final of the Turkish Prime Minister's Cup in 1958, the two clubs decided to share the cup ... and cut it down the middle.

That illustrates the passion, the imagination and the acquisitive ambition central to the Galatasaray Sports Club which administer not only professional football, but boast a wealth of other facilities. The club even own their own island in the Bosphorus straits equipped with its own swimming pool, boathouse, restaurant, discotheque and casino.

But it is football which draws the greatest crowds who, in turn, exert enormous pressure on coach, Fatih Terim, and his players. Terim, a former international defender, is only the ninth Turk to coach Galatasaray out of 42 trainers in the club's history. These have included 12 Englishmen, three Germans and two Scots – including Fatih's predecessor, Graeme Souness.

Only in recent years, however, have the club invested in a significant number of foreign players to underscore their ambitions to become a major force within the European club game.

Now Fatih has at his command not merely the pick of the Turkish game, but some world-famous imports – such as goalkeeper Claudio Taffarel, who was Brazil's hero when they defeated Italy in the only penalty shoot-out in World Cup Final history in Pasadena in 1994.

In front of him the defence is padlocked by Turkish strongman Bulent Korkmaz and marshalled by Romanian Gheorghe Popescu who captained Barcelona – under Bobby Robson – to European Cup-winners' Cup success in 1997.

Gheorghe Hagi: a wealth of success and experience.

An even more gifted Romanian runs midfield in the shape of Gheorghe Hagi, the greatest player in his country's history. Hagi was a teenage superstar with Sportul Studentesc and then army club Steaua Bucharest in the late 1980s. He was the midfield fulcrum of the Romanian national team who reached the quarter-finals of the 1994 World Cup and his magical left foot swirled a string of goals – some from "normal" play, many from free kicks – past many of the world's finest goalkeepers.

Spells at Real Madrid, Barcelona and in Italian football helped provide Hagi with an inspirational aura far beyond the achievement of almost any other eastern European footballer of modern times. Now reaping the benefit from such support at Galatasaray are winger Arif Erdem and centre-forward Hakan Sukur, the most outstanding product of the modern domestic game.

Arif hit headlines across Europe in this autumn's European Championship qualifying competition when he scored one of the fastest international hat-tricks of all time – hitting three goals in four minutes against Northern Ireland.

As for Hakan, he has been a hero of Turkish fans ever since his goals propelled the national team to the clsoing stages of the 1996 European Championship. It was the first time in more than 40 years that Turkey had reached the finals of any international competition.

But then, the fans expect the best for a club of Galatasaray's history and tradition. They were, for example, the first Turkish club to play abroad when they visited Hungary for a friendly against Kaposvar after domestic competition had been interrupted by the 1911–12 Balkan Wars. The club have won the league championship 13 times – a record they share with Fenerbahce – and the domestic cup on a record 12 occasions.

Fatih, not surprisingly perhaps for a former central defender, prefers the tactical security of the 4-4-2 system, but with both fullbacks, Fatih Aykel and Hakan Unsal, permitted freedom to attack whenever the opportunity presents itself. But the coach insists his players put team discipline before individual prowess.

He says: "I don't want any one player to be the key man. Then a team can be controlled too easily. For me, it is the system we play which is most important. Even the greatest players need a proper tactical foundation on which to make the skills count. If we work hard on the pitch then, hopefully, we can enjoy the rewards later."

Galatasaray Records

Record European victory: 5–0 v Neuchatel Xamax, European Cup 2nd round 1988–89

Record European defeat: 0–6 v Bayern Munich, European Cup 1st round 1972–73

Club records: Metin Oktay (608 matches and 211 goals)

Record scorer in Europe: Hakan Sukur, 17

Record attendance: 30,000 (international record)

Squad List

No.	Name	Date of birth	Position	Nationality	Domestic apps/goals	European Cup apps/goals
1	**Claudio Andre TAFFAREL**	08.05.1966	Goalkeeper	Brazil	– / –	14 / 0
12	**MEHMET Bolukbasi**	24.08.1978	Goalkeeper	Turkey	– / –	0 / 0
30	**Kerem INAN**	25.03.1980	Goalkeeper	Turkey	– / –	0 / 0
3	**BULENT Korkmaz**	24.11.1968	Defender	Turkey	– / –	52 / 1
4	**Gheorghe "GICA" POPESCU**	09.10.1967	Defender	Romania	– / –	46 / 3
14	**FAITH Akyel**	26.12.1977	Defender	Turkey	– / –	16 / 2
17	**Emrah EREN**	13.11.1978	Defender	Turkey	0 / 0	
33	**HAKAN UNSAL**	14.05.1973	Defender	Turkey	– / –	20 / 2
35	**Carlos Alberto De Oliveira "CAPONE"**	23.05.1972	Defender	Brazil	– / –	2 / 0
2	**Bruno EVERTON Quadros**	03.02.1977	Midfielder	Brazil	– / –	0 / 0
5	**EMRE Belozoglu**	07.09.1980	Midfielder	Turkey	– / –	7 / 0
7	**OKAN Buruk**	19.10.1973	Midfielder	Turkey	– / –	26 / 3
8	**SUAT Kaya**	26.08.1967	Midfielder	Turkey	– / –	26 / 2
10	**Gheorghe "GICA" HAGI**	05.02.1965	Midfielder	Romania	– / –	50 / 18
15	**Faruk ATALAY**	18.03.1981	Midfielder	Turkey	– / –	0 / 0
16	**Ahmet YILDIRIM**	25.04.1974	Midfielder	Turkey	– / –	3 / 0
20	**TUGAY Kerimoglu**	24.08.1970	Midfielder	Turkey	– / –	49 / 3
22	**UMIT Davala**	30.07.1973	Midfielder	Turkey	– / –	19 / 1
67	**ERGUN Pembe**	17.05.1972	Midfielder	Turkey	– / –	21 / 1
6	**ARIF Erdem**	02.01.1972	Forward	Turkey	– / –	46 / 10
9	**HAKAN SUKUR**	01.09.1971	Forward	Turkey	– / –	43 / 17
11	**Saffet AKYUZ**	11.03.1970	Forward	Turkey	– / –	2 / 1
18	**Mehmet YOZGATLI**	09.01.1979	Forward	Turkey	– / –	1 / 1
23	**HASAN Sas Gokhan**	01.08.1976	Forward	Turkey	– / –	8 / 0
24	**BURAK Akdis**	12.06.1977	Forward	Turkey	– / –	1 / 0
36	**Mandinga dos Santos MARCIO**	23.01.1975	Forward	Brazil	– / –	0 / 0

Formed 1892 **Coach** Jurgen Rober **Stadium** Olympiastadion **Capacity** 75,729 **Address** Hans-Braun-Strasse, Friesenhaus 2, 14053 Berlin **Website** www.herthabsc.de

Hertha Berlin

HERTHA have come a long way in three years – from the brink of dropping out of the professional game to the competitive pinnacle of world club football.

But then, Hertha are a unique club because they play in a city with a remarkable history. West Berlin was, of course, an island in the middle of Soviet-dominated eastern Europe for more than 40 years. Imagine London without a single Premier League club or without a representative in a European competition for 20 years.

That was the fate of West Berlin football – not only during the years in which walls both political and physical divided the city. Long after the reunification of East and West Germany and the dismantling of the old border posts and "Transit Berlin" autobahn signs, Hertha were on the brink of extinction.

Only four months after the arrival of coach Jurgen Rober in January 1996, they were one game away from relegation back to the ranks of the regional amateur leagues where the club had spent depressing years in the late 1970s and again in the 1980s. Their average crowd was 3,000 in the crumbling Olympic stadium which had once hosted 110,000 to see Jesse Owens win the long jump at the infamous 1936 Olympic Games.

Rober says: "Nobody in the city wanted to know the club then. We were a team without any credit even in our own city. Newspapers wrote only bad things – if they wrote anything at all. Now people see something is happening. They read good things about us. Suddenly they think we must win everything."

The man whose managerial tutors from his playing days included Brian Clough at Nottingham Forest, has worked a miracle. In the past three seasons Rober has guided Hertha to promotion back into the Bundesliga and then brought them into the Champions League thanks to last season's third-place finish. Success brought back the fans. In those three years the average attendance leaped to 52,182 last season with the Olympic Stadium full to its new domestic capacity of nearly 76,000 on three occasions.

But Rober acknowledges that the club still have a long way to go. Hopefully, the interest and income generated by the Champions League will act as a catalyst – enabling the club to expand a tightly controlled backroom staff and buy players comfortable on the international stage.

The present squad includes 11 foreign players, but only two who featured in the 1998 World Cup finals – Iran forward Ali Daei and versatile Norwergian Kjetil Rekdal. Similarly, Hertha boast only three German internationals and not one of them featured in the World Cup squad at France '98.

Rober says: "It's true, there are few stars. Our success has

Kjetil Rekdal: one of only two Hertha players at France '98.

been achieved as a team. For us it is a learning experience. That is all."

Of course, Hertha fans thrilled by accession to the Champions League expect much more than Rober – they want an achievement appropriate for the year in which the city of Berlin regains its status as seat of the German government. In the first home Bundesliga match of the season, they whistled and jeered because Hertha only drew with German Cup-holders, Werder Bremen.

All Rober's careful planning was then undermined by an injury crisis. Sports director, Dieter Hoeness, immediately signed veteran defender, Thomas Helmer, to shore up defence. Helmer, released by Bayern Munich at the end of last season, had moved to England to experience the Premiership with Sunderland, but he was delighted to come home, after less than two months, and find himself back in the Champions League.

Behind Helmer in goal is Hungary keeper Gabor Kiraly, now in his third season in Berlin since arriving from Haladas Szombathely. Rekdal, though originally a winger or midfielder, has moved back to help organise a defence which has been strengthened by the summer signing of German international, Marko Rehmer, from Hansa Rostock.

Dariusz Wosz and Andreas Thom are midfielders with international experience for both the former East Germany and the unified Germany. They provide the attacking opportunities for Michael Preetz, the Bundesliga's 23-goal top scorer last term, and new signing Sebastian Deisler from Borussia Monchengladbach – the so-called "German Beckham".

If only Hertha's version of the Manchester United star could emulate his success!

Hertha Berlin Records

European honours: None

Record European victory: 4–0 v Esbjerg, UEFA Cup 3rd round 1978–79

Record European defeat: 1–4 v Ajax Amsterdam, UEFA Cup 2nd round 1975–76

Club records: Michael Sziedat (280 Bundesliga matches), Erich Beer (83 Bundesliga goals)

Record scorer in Europe: Lorenz Horr, 10

Record attendance: 88,705 (v 1. FC Koln, September 26th, 1969)

Squad List

No.	Name	Date of birth	Position	Nationality	Domestic apps/goals	European Cup apps/goals
1	**Gabor KIRALY**	01.04.1976	Goalkeeper	Hungary	65 / 0	2 / 0
12	**Christian FIEDLER**	27.03.1975	Goalkeeper	Germany	7 / 0	0 / 0
2	**Hendrik HERZOG**	02.04.1969	Defender	Germany	174 / 13	9 / 0
4	**Dick VAN BURIK**	29.11.1973	Defender	Holland	49 / 1	0 / 0
6	**Eyjulfur SVERRISSON**	03.08.1968	Defender	Iceland	168 / 26	13 / 1
10	**Kjetil REKDAL**	06.11.1968	Defender	Norway	59 / 4	5 / 1
33	**Marko REHMER**	29.04.1972	Defender	Germany	81 / 4	0 / 0
34	**Thomas HELMER**	21.04.1965	Defender	Germany	387 / 40	43 / 7
5	**Kostas KONSTANTINIDIS**	31.08.1972	Midfielder	Greece	4 / 0	11 / 0
8	**Dariusz WOSZ**	08.06.1969	Midfielder	Germany	181 / 23	10 / 1
15	**Bryan ROY**	12.02.1970	Midfielder	Holland	0 / 0	19 / 2
16	**Sixten VEIT**	07.01.1970	Midfielder	Germany	55 / 5	1 / 0
17	**Anthony SANNEH**	01.06.1971	Midfielder	USA	6 / 0	1 / 0
18	**Pal DARDAI**	16.03.1976	Midfielder	Hungary	39 / 2	3 / 0
19	**Andreas SCHMIDT**	14.09.1973	Midfielder	Germany	62 / 6	2 / 0
20	**Andreas NEUENDORF**	09.02.1975	Midfielder	Germany	62 / 4	1 / 0
21	**Michael HARTMANN 1**	01.07.1974	Midfielder	Germany	39 / 2	2 / 0
23	**Rene TRETSCHOK**	23.12.1968	Midfielder	Germany	130 / 21	21 /
24	**Kai MICHALKE**	05.04.1976	Midfielder	Germany	88 / 11	2 / 0
26	**Sebastian DEISLER**	05.01.1980	Midfielder	Germany	20 / 3	1 / 0
27	**Andreas THOM**	07.09.1965	Midfielder	Germany	203 / 42	38 / 13
9	**Ali DAEI**	21.03.1969	Forward	Iran	52 / 14	6 / 1
11	**Michael PREETZ**	17.08.1967	Forward	Germany	130 / 44	1 / 1
22	**Piotr REISS**	20.06.1972	Forward	Poland	10 / 1	0 / 0
25	**Ilija ARACIC**	15.11.1970	Forward	Croatia	16 / 6	2 / 0

Formed 1899 **Coach** Alberto Zaccheroni **Stadium** Giuseppe Meazza **Capacity** 85,700 **Address** Via Turati 3, 20121 Milano **Website** www.acmilan.it

Milan

TO win this season's expanded Champions League means playing a staggering 17 games and the only clubs likely to stand a chance are those with large squads.

Milan may have squeezed their way to their 16th Italian league title right at the death and are perhaps not the feared unit they once were. Indeed, after a difficult transition, they are back in Europe for the first time in three years. But tradition and overall strength suggest they should not be taken lightly.

The key to success is never sitting still and coach Alberto Zaccheroni, who arrived from Udinese in July, 1998, made two significant signings which he hopes will help pave the way to Champions League success. Brazilian wing-back, Serginho, arrived from Sao Paolo for £7 million while Andryi Shevchenko, hailed as the new Marco Van Basten, was bought from Dynamo Kiev for £16 million.

Traditionally, Italian teams are at their most impenetrable in defence, but this season Milan look more capable in attack than they do at the back. Alongside Schevchenko, they have Oliver Bierhoff, the German international striker whose goals played a huge part in helping Milan to last season's Scudetto. Throw George Weah, the mercurial Liberian and one of Africa's finest exports, into the equation and you have an attack bristling with talent and quality. Ironically, it is in defence where Milan may come unstuck.

They have plenty of experience, certainly, but one wonders whether Paulo Maldini and Alberto Costacurta, with a combined age of 64, will be able to cope with the quickfire attacks of the opposition and a long, gruelling programme that stretches well into next spring.

And yet, history suggests that the red and black side of the famous northern Italian footballing city will take some stopping, especially as they are celebrating their centenary this year. All you have to do is look back at the competition to understand what it means to the fans. Milan have won Europe's most prestigious club competition five times, beginning in 1963 with a 2–1 win over Benfica. Six years later, Ajax were the fall guys as Milan trounced the Dutchmen 4–1 in Madrid.

Andryi Shevchenko: a £7 million summer signing hailed as the "new" Van Basten.

Squad List

No.	Name	Date of birth	Position	Nationality	Domestic apps/goals	European Cup apps/goals
1	**Sebastiano ROSSI**	20.07.1964	Goalkeeper	Italy	315 / 0	40 / 0
12	**Christian ABBIATI**	08.07.1977	Goalkeeper	Italy	18 / 0	0 / 0
40	**Valerio FIORI**	27.04.1969	Goalkeeper	Italy	228 / 0	10 / 0
3	**Paolo MALDINI**	26.06.1968	Defender	Italy	403 / 21	70 / 2
5	**Alessandro COSTACURTA**	24.04.1966	Defender	Italy	320 / 2	64 / 0
14	**Roberto Fabian AYALA**	11.04.1973	Defender	Argentina	98 / 1	0 / 0
25	**Bruno N'GOTTY**	10.06.1971	Defender	France	25 / 1	26 / 2
26	**Luigi SALA**	21.02.1974	Defender	Italy	80 / 3	0 / 0
28	**Mirco SADOTTI**	18.05.1975	Defender	Italy	0 / 0	0 / 0
36	**Michele FERRI**	29.05.1981	Defender	Italy	0 / 0	0 / 0
2	**Thomas HELVEG**	24.06.1971	Midfielder	Denmark	139 / 5	11 / 0
4	**Demetrio ALBERTINI**	23.08.1971	Midfielder	Italy	231 / 20	41 / 3
8	**Gennaro Ivan GATTUSO**	09.01.1978	Midfielder	Italy	33 / 0	7 / 2
15	**Diego DE ASCENTIS**	31.07.1976	Midfielder	Italy	55 / 3	0 / 0
16	**Max TONETTO**	18.11.1974	Midfielder	Italy	81 / 4	0 / 0
19	**Pierluigi ORLANDINI**	09.10.1972	Midfielder	Italy	121 / 15	9 / 0
21	**Federico GIUNTI**	06.08.1971	Midfielder	Italy	51 / 4	1 / 0
23	**Massimo AMBROSINI**	29.05.1977	Midfielder	Italy	71 / 2	14 / 1
24	**Andres GUGLIELMINPIETRO 'GIULY'**	10.04.1974	Midfielder	Argentina	21 / 4	0 / 0
27	**Sergio 'SERGINHO' Dos Santos**	27.06.1971	Midfielder	Brazil	0 / 0	0 / 0
34	**Simonluca AGAZZONE**	23.07.1981	Midfielder	Italy	0 / 0	0 / 0
7	**Andriy SHEVCHENKO**	29.09.1976	Forward	Ukraine	0 / 0	29 / 19
9	**George WEAH**	01.10.1966	Forward	Liberia	103 / 42	53 / 30
10	**Zvonimir BOBAN**	08.10.1968	Forward	Croatia	162 / 15	41 / 8
11	**Maurizio GANZ**	13.10.1968	Forward	Italy	175 / 57	16 / 10
18	**LEONARDO Nascimento Araujo**	05.09.1969	Forward	Brazil	54 / 15	12 / 3
20	**Oliver BIERHOFF**	01.05.1968	Forward	Germany	137 / 79	4 / 2
32	**Andrea RABITO**	11.05.1980	Forward	Italy	0 / 0	0 / 0

In those years, Milan boasted some of the greatest players to represent any Italian side in Europe. Gianni Rivera was the golden boy, the idol of the tifosi – having cost a then-sensational £65,000 as a 16 year-old back in 1961. Rivera replaced England's controversial Jimmy Greaves and masterminded Milan's triumphs through the 1960s and early 1970s. Brazil's Jose Altafini and Angelo Sormani, Sweden's Kurt Hamrin and Italy's own Pierino Prati were just a handful of the star strikers for whom Rivera opened the way to goal time and time again.

Although Milan continued to pick up other European prizes, they had to wait another generation before they could collect the most coveted title for a third time. Back-to-back victories over Steaua Bucharest and Benfica showed the whole of Europe that Milan were, once again, the Continent's most feared fighting force, but nothing, before or after, could quite match their victory in 1994 over Barcelona.

On paper, there was little to choose between the two vast footballing empires, but on a May evening in Athens, Milan, inspired by Marco van Basten, swept aside the Catalan giants 4–0 with one of the most sublime performances ever seen in European club football. Many said it was akin to Real Madrid's famous 7–3 victory over Eintracht Frankfurt back in the 1960s. The arguments will go on and on, but one thing is for sure – Milan's return to the top flight can only enhance the Champions League.

Milan Records

European honours: European Cup 1962–63, 1968–69, 1988–89, 1989–90, 1993–94; Cup-winners' Cup 1967–68, 1972–73.

Record European victory: 8–0 v Union Luxembourg, European Cup 1st round 1962–63

Record European defeat: 1–5 v Barcelona, European Cup 2nd round 1959–60

Club records: Gianni Rivera (501 league matches), Gunnar Nordahl (210 goals)

Record scorer in Europe: Jose Altafini, 20

Record attendance: 78,650 (v AS Monaco April 27th, 1994)

3 Last Season

THE final of the world's greatest international club competition had never seen anything like May 1999 as Manchester United grabbed two goals in time added on to defeat Bayern Munich in Barcelona.

United's achievement of the treble of UEFA Champions League, domestic league and FA Cup (matching the feats of Celtic, Ajax and PSV Eindhoven) was completed with the incredible drama of 94 utterly unforgettable minutes in Barcelon's Nou Camp stadium. United, their fans, and even manager Alex (later, Sir Alex) Ferguson, could barely believe it, neither could Bayern. In the moments that followed referee Pierluigi Collina's final whistle Ferguson looked almost as dazed and shell-shocked as Bayern boss Ottmar Hitzfeld.

"You know, this would have been Sir Matt Busby's 90th birthday today. Well, perhaps he was up there kicking a lot for us tonight." - Manchester United manager Sir Alex Ferguson after victory over Bayern Munich in Barcelona.

The difference was that Hitzfeld continued to look shell-shocked as the cup presentation took place. Ferguson quickly emerged from his stupor, saying: "I didn't like most of the match, but the most important thing it showed was that you can never deny our people's spirit and will to win. That's what won it for us.

"In the closing minutes I had been preparing myself mentally for defeat – thinking that maybe it wasn't our year and I would need to keep my dignity. Then, well ... at the final whistle I was just stunned. I didn't say anything

Last season's final was a night to remember, not only for Alex Ferguson but for every football fan.

An historic treble for Manchester United was won and celebrated in style.

to the players. I just hugged and kissed them, slavered all over them.

"It was the greatest moment of my life."

By the time the Final came round, few observers had any doubts that the right teams had progressed to Nou Camp. Oddly enough, both Bayern and United had been drawn in the same first round group when the Germans finished with their noses in front, pipping United to top spot by one point. United progressed to the quarter-finals courtesy of the complex qualifying system – the six groups sending each section's winning club through to the quarter-finals plus the two runner-up clubs with the best comparative records.

At least United were in exalted company in qualifying through the back door – so did reigning Cup-holders Real Madrid from Group C which was won by Internazionale of Milan. Olympiakos of Greece qualified as winners of Group A. Juventus from Group B – though Juventus were not sure of reaching the quarter-finals until the final whistle of their last group match. It took a detailed study of the rules and regulations to place them ahead of Turkey's Galatasaray and Norway's Rosenborg after all three clubs finished on eight points.

There was no such tight finish for Dynamo Kiev in Group E. The attacking power of Andryi Shevchenko and Sergiy Rebrov meant that they finished a comfortable three points clear of Lens and Arsenal. Kaiserslautern had an even easier time of it in Group F – the "other" German entrants finished five points in front of Benfica.

The quarter-finals produced a flurry of drama. Two goals from £12 million, new signing Dwight Yorke earned United a home win over Inter that the Italians could not overturn back in Milan. But holders Madrid lost their crown as they went down 1–1 and then 0–2 against Kiev. Real Madrid were always struggling to raise both form and morale after replacing coach Guus Hiddink with John Toshack shortly before the tie.

Juventus squeaked through against Olympiakos with an 85th-minute away goal from Antonio Conte in the second leg, handing them the away-goal advantage. As for the all-German clash, Bayern had fewer problems than they feared seeing off Kaiserslautern –

Olympiakos were just edged out by Juventus.

winning 2–0 at home and by a masterful 4–0 away.

Nerves got the better of Kaiserslautern in front of their own fans; they never recovered after the eighth-minute expulsion of their Hungarian central defender, Janos Hrutka.

United appeared on their way out after being held 1–1 by Juventus at Old Trafford in the first leg of the semi-final. But manager Alex Ferguson said he was confident United would score in Turin. Not only did they score, but they secured a sensational 3–2 win after Juventus had seized an early 2–0 lead with goals from Filippo Inzaghi.

"After that performance I can say only that Manchester deserve to win the Cup itself," said Juventus coach Carlo Ancelotti, generous in defeat.

Bayern, of course, had other ideas after beating Kiev 4–3 on aggregate (3–3 and then 1–0). The Germans had goalkeeper Oliver Kahn to thank for a string of superb saves in the second leg in Munich. He held Shevchenko and Co. at bay just long enough for Mario Basler to snatch a breakaway goal for Bayern at the other end. After that 36th-minute strike, Kiev faded and Bayern strode into the Final.

Both finalists were under strength for the big event. United missed suspended skipper Roy Keane, while Bayern lacked injured top scorer, Giovane Elber, and French World Cup-winning leftback, Bixente Lizarazu. Ferguson, controversially, covered for Keane by moving Beckham inside from the right wing and switching Ryan Giggs from left to right flank.

United fans outnumbered Bayern supporters by around 10-to-1 yet it was United who appeared the more nervy in the opening exchanges – outgoing goalkeeper Peter Schmeichel especially. A couple of fluffed clearances encouraged Bayern and they duly went ahead in the sixth minute through Mario Basler's low, curling free kick after Ronny Johnsen had brought down Carsten Jancker just outside the penalty box.

The gamble of switching Beckham inside meant United appeared short of defensive responsibility in midfield. This could have proved costly in the 13th minute when no-one picked up veteran Lothar Matthaus as he ambled forward on to a short free kick from Stefan Effenberg in midfield. Fortunately for United, Matthaus's angled chip aimed at Jancker carried slightly too much pace.

The rest of the first half was predictable with United trying to force the pace. Andy Cole could not punish a loose ball bobbing around the Bayern penalty box, and a back-flipped header from Yorke forced a clumsy flap of a save from Kahn. At the other end, Schmeichel and his team-mates allowed Matthaus more freedom to dash forward, but Alexander Zickler dragged his subsequent shot wide.

Half time arrived leaving Ferguson with a tactical puzzle as well as the goal deficit to ponder. He appeared to have sacrificed the best that his team had to offer by using his wide men in just that role – wide but not wide enough. Giggs, on the right, was forced to keep cutting inside, as did an under-performing Jesper Blomqvist from out on the left. They appeared to be playing into Bayern's hands.

United stuck with their game plan for the start of the second half, yet it was Bayern who came closer to scoring. First, Jancker went round Schmeichel, but allowed the keeper to recover and concede a corner; then Effenberg fired narrowly wide before forcing a fine save from the Dane. Bayern grew even more dangerous as substitute Mehmet Scholl brought his fresh legs and undoubted skills into play. In the 79th minute he chipped against a post.

By now United, with striker substitutes Teddy Sheringham and Ole Gunnar Solskjaer on the field, were risking gaps at the back in the desperate battle to conjure up an equaliser. Twice more, Bayern very nearly capitalised. Scholl forced another sharp save from Schmeichel, and then Jancker's overhead effort hit the bar.

Time was running out for United as assistant referee Fiorenzo Treossi held up the illuminated board signalling three minutes of extra time. The board was red, as if for danger, but Bayern failed to notice. In the last minute of the 90 United forced a corner. Schmeichel charged up field, exacerbating the penalty box chaos. Effenberg hooked out the loose ball, Giggs drilled it back in and Sheringham turned it inside Kahn's right-hand post for the equaliser.

Bayern's defenders looked distraught, but worse was to come. Within two minutes United had forced Sammi Kuffour into conceding another corner. Beckham curled it in, Sheringham headed on and Solskjaer stabbed the ball up into the roof of the net.

Bedlam erupted all around the ground. A sensational finish, a fairytale recovery, a professional miracle. For the second time in their history, Manchester United were kings of Europe – and the Treble turned Alex Ferguson into a knight football will never forget.

Germany's third club: Kaiserslautern's Marion Hristov attacks against Helsinki.

(Overleaf): The moment that sent shockwaves around Europe as Solskjaer seals victory for Manchester United.

PlayStation

4 History

IT ALL started on September 4, 1955, in Lisbon where a crowd of 60,000 saw Sporting Clube de Portugal draw 3–3 with Partizan of Belgrade. Four days later Real Madrid set their own ball rolling when they defeated Servette 2–0 in Switzerland. Appropriately it was Madrid's right half and captain – and later long-serving coach – Miguel Munoz, who scored their first goal.

The European Champion Clubs' Cup, now the UEFA Champions League, had come to life.

This was football in a different era. Television was a new technological toy which caught fading images of the first final, but nothing else. But the glamour of Real Madrid, winning for the first five years in a row, provided the magical lustre which launched the European Champion Clubs' Cup on its journey into the sporting stratosphere.

The first final was staged in the old Parc des Princes in Paris. French champions Reims raced into a lead of 2–0 then 3–1, but Real Madrid stormed back to win 4–3. Their Argentine-born centre-forward, Alfredo Di Stefano, inside forward compatriot, Hector Rial, and flying left winger, Francisco Gento, were on their way towards football immortality.

The next season, the English joined up in the shape of Manchester United's "Busby Babes". They opened with a 10–0 thrashing of Belgian champions Anderlecht but were ultimately too inexperienced to cope with the semi-final sophistication of Madrid – who retained the Cup by defeating Italy's Fiorentina 2–0 in the Final.

Next season, 1957–58, was overshadowed by tragedy after a quarter-final in which Manchester United had scored a thrilling victory over Red Star Belgrade. Their plane crashed on take-off after a refuelling stop in Munich on the way home. Eight players were killed, including England stalwarts Roger Byrne, Duncan Edwards and Tommy Taylor. A weakened United duly lost in the semi-finals to Milan who were, in turn, unable to prevent Madrid completing a hat-trick in the Final.

In 1958–59 Reims returned to the attack with a forward line spearheaded by Just Fontaine, who had scored a record-breaking 13 goals at the World Cup finals in Sweden. Even he could not find a chink in Madrid's armour as Reims lost again in the Final to the Spanish giants, this time by 2–0.

A year later Madrid exemplified all the class, excitement and drama of the European Cup in the most famous match in its history. Indeed, their 7–3 demolition of Eintracht Frankfurt at Hampden Park, Glasgow, in May, 1960, is often hailed as the greatest match of all time. Di Stefano scored three of Madrid's goals with the other four all contributed by the great Hungarian Ferenc Puskas.

The end of an era

Yet that was also the beginning of the end. Madrid were eliminated in the second round the following season by their Spanish rivals, Barcelona – led by a veteran Hungarian of their own in Ladislav Kubala and by possibly the greatest Spanish footballer of all time in Luis Suarez. The Catalans were favourites for the final in Bern, but Portuguese outsiders Benfica of Lisbon played magnificently to win 3–2 after Barcelona hit both posts and crossbar.

For the following season, 1961–62, Benfica reinforced their attack in formidable fashion with the addition of their new Mozambique-born striker, Eusebio. His presence proved enough to help tilt the scales Benfica's way in a thrilling semi-final win over Tottenham Hotspur. Then he struck twice in a wonderful 5–3 victory over the old masters

Zarrago holds aloft the trophy for Real in 1959.

Madrid in the Final.

The 1962–63 season saw a first Italian success as Milan overthrew Benfica 2–1 in the first Final to be staged at Wembley. But the nature of football was changing. The free-flowing attacking football of the 1950s had given way to a much more pragmatic, physical style.

Helenio Herrera's Internazionale of Milan were the most adept and ruthless exponents of this negative, new, counter-attacking football. Inter had bought Luis Suarez from Barcelona to run midfield and revealed the youthful Sandro Mazzola – the equal of Rivera – in attack. In 1963 they had too much strength for an ageing, fading Madrid. Mazzola scored two of Inter's goals in a 3–1 win to finish as the competition's seven-goal co-top scorer.

Liverpool made their mark on the Champions Cup scene, announcing their arrival in 1964–65 by reaching the semi-finals. They even harboured brief ambitions of beating Inter in the semi-finals. But, after winning 3–1 at home, Liverpool were outmanoeuvred in Milan. Inter's Spanish forward, Joaquin Peiro, "stole" a bounced ball from keeper Tommy Lawrence for one goal and attacking fullback, Giacinto Facchetti, scored a brilliant winner. In the Final, also staged in the San Siro, Inter beat Benfica 1–0.

A rejuvenated Real Madrid made a brief winning comeback in 1966 before British football celebrated its first European champions a year later. Surprisingly, it was not Manchester United or Liverpool who secured the prize, but Scotland's Celtic after defeating Inter 2–1 in Lisbon's National Stadium. Manager Jock Stein's men overcame the shock of an early penalty by Mazzola to win with storming second-half goals from Tommy Gemmell and Stevie Chalmers.

British domination was extended the following season when Manchester United – amid high emotion – marked the 10th anniversary of the Munich air disaster by defeating Benfica to win the trophy their predecessors had been pursuing. Benfica resisted bravely against United and the pressure of the Wembley crowd for the first 90 minutes of the Final and only a remarkable late save by goalkeeper Alex Stepney from Eusebio earned United extra time. Then, however, their superior fitness and ambition lifted them to three further goals and a 4–1 win. Munich survivor Bobby Charlton scored twice.

Yet United's reign lasted less than a year. Milan beat them in the 1969 semi-finals and then thrashed a naive, youthful Ajax Amsterdam 4–1 in the Final in Madrid.

With hindsight, however, Milan's success was less significant than Ajax's presence in the Final. A year later Feyenoord became the first Dutch champions of Europe when they defeated Celtic 2–1 in extra-time in Milan. Then Ajax themselves embarked upon the three-year run in which they enthralled the world game. Ajax's so-called "total football" was perhaps the ultimate expression of modern soccer – involving footballers of high technical and intellectual competence switching and inter-changing to suit the state of the game. All of it was threaded together by the central genius of Johan Cruyff who starred in the 2–0 win over Panathinaikos in 1971 then scored both goals when Ajax beat Inter 2–0 in the 1972 Final.

Next season, 1972–73, was Ajax's swansong, but only after they had become the first club since Real Madrid to win the Champions Cup three years running. This they achieved thanks to a 1–0 win over Juventus in the Final – a game which was not as close as the scoreline might suggest. Ajax scored through Johnny Rep after only four minutes and played such wonderful, sweeping football over the next quarter of an hour that they could have won by a hatful of goals. It was almost as if they became bored with their own domination.

No German team had, up to now, won the Champions Cup, but in 1973–74 the Ajax bubble burst after Cruyff was sold to Barcelona for a world-record £922,000. Franz Beckenbauer's Bayern Munich immediately took over their crown – though not without difficulty. Bayern needed the only replay in European Cup Final history before despatching Atletico Madrid 4–0, with two goals apiece from Uli Hoeness and Gerd Muller.

Bayern retained the Cup in 1975, but the Final was marred by the first major eruption of a decade of English hooligan violence in Europe. The angry fans of Leeds United ripped out seats and seat backs in the new Parc des Princes in Paris in the closing minutes of their 2–0 defeat. Bayern then went on to complete a hat-trick of their own by squeezing past Saint-Etienne 1–0 the following year.

Spain, Portugal, Italy, Holland and Germany had all enjoyed their eras of dominance.

English teams dominate

Now it was the turn of Engish football – starting with Liverpool in 1977. Under Shankly and then Bob Paisley, Liverpool had been irresistible for more than a decade in England. It had been only a question of time before they translated that into Champions Cup success by defeating Borussia Monchengladbach 3–1 in Rome in what was Kevin Keegan's competitive farewell before his transfer to Hamburg.

Liverpool went marching on a year later. They replaced Keegan with the even better Kenny Dalglish from Celtic and he duly scored the goal with which Liverpool defeated Belgium's Brugge in the 1978 Final.

Liverpool's second defence was short-lived, upset in the autumn of 1978 by Brian Clough's Nottingham Forest. Clough had become a football cult figure in England. His idiosyncratic style was never appreciated on the continent, but Forest's two successive Champions Cup victories – first by 1-0 over Malmo,

A British first: Celtic's Billy McNeil in 1967.

Ajax's Johan Cryuff (left) with team-mate Hulshoff Barry celebrate after beating Juventus in 1973.

then Hamburg – ensured his place in football legend.

The Cup stayed in England for a fifth successive year in 1981 when Liverpool beat Real Madrid 1–0 (yet again) and then Aston Villa maintained the English grip in 1982. Villa beat Bayern in the Final with a goal from centre-forward Peter Withe – who very nearly fell over his own feet before toe-poking the ball home from inside the six-yard box.

Bayern had been favourites against Aston Villa, but such a role has often weighed too heavily. The Athens Final of 1983 underlined the point once more since the galaxy of superstars from Juventus – including Frenchman Michel Platini, Poland's Zbigniew Boniek and Italy's own Paolo Rossi – had been expected to run rings around the workmen of Hamburg. Instead, a lone goal from from Hamburg midfielder Felix Magath proved decisive.

Hamburg's victory was not, however, the precursor of a German revival – just a blip on the Anglo-Italian screen. The 1983–84 season saw Liverpool return in triumph to Rome's Olympic stadium, scene of their 1977 triumph. This time they had the audacity to defeat hosts Roma in a penalty shoot-out.

Disaster at Heysel

Liverpool returned to the Final again in 1985. They lost 1–0 to Juventus and the occasion is frequently called to mind ... but never for the football. May 29, 1985, was the day of the Heysel stadium disaster when 39 Juventus fans were killed, crushed against or falling through a weak retaining wall after being charged across the terracing by a hooligan mob. It was a horrific international display of the evils of hooliganism and the awful scenes were beamed around the world by the television cameras present to broadcast what should have been the glories of European club football's most prestigious match.

Criminal charges were laid against Belgian and UEFA officials and video film was used to track down some of the hooligans. Controversy surrounded UEFA's decision to go ahead with the match amid such carnage, but it did keep the remainder of the crowd in the stadium, preventing more trouble on the streets of Brussels and not clogging up traffic lanes cleared for the emergency services.

The match was decided by a penalty converted by Michel Platini, but this was not a night to be remembered with pride and provoked the removal of English clubs from Europe for five long years.

Yet, oddly, in the first post-Heysel season there was an English presence in the Champions Cup Final in Barcelona's coach, Terry Venables. Barcelona reached the 1986 Final believing that they needed merely to turn up to win. The venue was also Spanish, the Sanchez Pizjuan stadium in Seville, and their opposition were the underrated, little-appreciated Steaua of Bucharest. On the night, however, Barcelona's attack was swallowed up by a Romanian defence superbly marshalled by Miodrag Belodedici. Even when it went to a penalty shoot-out Barsa could not put the ball in the net. Steaua duly made history by 3–0.

In 1987, FC Porto became the first Portuguese club since Benfica 25 years earlier to win the Champions Cup when they hit back with style and panache to defeat Bayern Munich 2–1, but they proved out of luck a year later – losing on penalties to PSV Eindhoven after a goalless draw in Stuttgart.

PSV had been most observers' favourites for the trophy and the only surprise was that Benfica made them work so hard in the Final. This was, after all, the year in which a second generation of Dutch football achieved a European monopoly with PSV winning the Champions Cup and then the national team winning the European Championship in West Germany. PSV provided goalkeeper Van Breukelen, defenders Berry Van Aerle and Ronald Koeman as well as midfielder Gerald Vanenburg to the Dutch effort.

In the Final Koeman converted PSV's first kick in the penalty shoot-out while Van Breukelen saved the decisive, last, penalty taken by Benfica's Veloso. But this was not the beginning of a new Dutch era, at least, not directly.

In the mid-1980s, Milan, one of the original Champions Cup contestants back in 1955–56, had been taken over by the millionaire businessman and media magnate, Silvio Berlusconi. He was a long-standing fan of the club but, more, he had a grand commercial vision which would help reshape football as a business in its own right and as a commercial contributor.

Berlusconi poured £20 million into Milan initially to pay off the debts of the old regime and buy Dutch superstars Ruud Gullit and Marco Van Basten (joined a year later by Frank Rijkaard). Results were spectacular. In 1988 Milan won the Italian league and then they collected the Champions Cup two years in a row.

Milan were among the television stars of Berlusconi's electronic empire and he even flew in his own TV crews and equipment to Barcelona for the 1989 Final when Spanish technicians went on strike. His investment was rewarded with Milan's sweeping 4–0 victory over Steaua Bucharest. Gullit and Van Basten scored twice each. Rijkaard achieved his own moment of glory in 1990, scoring the Final winner against Benfica in Vienna.

By now the pressure of the occasion reduced most finalist teams to frightened rabbits. Both Yugoslavia's Red Star Belgrade and France's Marseille "froze" in a dire Final in Bari in 1991. Again it was 0–0 at the end of extra time and thus duly became the fourth Champions Cup Final decided on penalties. Manuel Amoros, experienced World Cup veteran, missed Marseille's first kick and Red Star converted all theirs to win 5–3. Sweeper Miodrag Belodedici thus became the first player to win the Cup with two different clubs, after having collected a winner's medal in 1986 with Steaua.

Another echo of 1986 was heard in 1992 when Barcelona, beaten finalists both then and back in 1961, achieved their long-awaited Champions Cup success. The Catalan giants had appeared jinxed in the one

Marseille's match-winner Basile Boli with the trophy in 1993.

Living up to history: Nothing less than a win in Europe is expected, but Real managed just that in 1998.

competition they wanted to win above all others. To succeed they had to negotiate safely a new mini-league structure which UEFA had dropped, experimentally, into the spring slot previously taken up by the quarter and semi-finals.

In Group B of the mini-league Barcelona triumphed over Sparta Prague, Benfica and Dynamo Kiev while Group A saw Italy's Sampdoria outrun Red Star Belgrade (now homeless in European competition because of the Yugoslav conflict), Anderlecht and Panathinaikos.

The Final, at Wembley, saw no goals in the 90 minutes despite some high-quality football. No need for penalties this time, though. Eight minutes before the end of extra-time Barcelona were awarded a free kick almost 30 yards from goal. One touch and Ronald Koeman thundered his drive beyond keeper Gianluca Pagliuca. Barcelona celebrated in style. They had brought their "real" kit to replace the change strip they had played in and it was in their traditional red and blue that they collected the Cup for which they had waited so long.

UEFA now formalised the mini-league system into the newly baptised Champions League. The European governing body had called a special meeting to reshape its statutes and secure authority to market the entire competition as it saw fit – with exclusive sponsorship and television contracts.

Rules and regulations played a role in the early rounds, too, when Stuttgart fielded one foreigner too many against Leeds. The English champions won the duly ordered replay then fell to Rangers – who went on into the Champions League. The Scottish champions very nearly reached the Final, too, but were pipped by Marseille, who duly went on to face Milan in Munich.

A goal from Basile Boli brought France their first-ever Champions Cup, but even that night whispers were circulating that Marseille's successes were not all they seemed. Ultimately it emerged that Marseille had fixed the league match before the Final, against Valenciennes, so that they could concentrate on facing Milan knowing that the French league title was once again safely theirs.

The ripples of corruption spread on down the years. Marseille were barred from defending their tarnished Cup, but it was not until the spring of 1997 that club president Bernard Tapie was jailed for match fixing. By then it had become clear that Marseille had fixed far, far more than just the infamous match with Valenciennes.

The credibility of the entire Champions Cup was on the linc in 1993–94. Milan rose to that challenge - defeating Barcelona 4–0 in Athens in the Final with one of the finest displays of football seen in the event for more than 20 years.

They did so, remarkably, despite the absences through suspension of key central defenders, Billy Costacurta and Franco Baresi, and the further absence, through injury, of spearhead Marco Van Basten. The exigencies of UEFA's foreigners rules meant, also, that coach Fabio Capello left Romania's Florian Raducioiu and Denmark's Brian Laudrup in the stand.

Barcelona, under Johan Cruyff, were renowned for some of the finest one-touch attacking football in Europe – their attack spearheaded by a fearsome partnership in Brazil's Romario and Bulgaria's Hristo Stoichkov.

Not that they ever saw much of the ball. Milan took the game by the scruff of the neck with Marcel Desailly providing the power and Dejan Savicevic all the skill and inspiration. Daniele Massaro (two), Savicevic and Desailly scored the goals.

Back from the wilderness

English clubs were, by now, back in Europe, but both they and their German cousins struggled to keep pace with the tactical and technical developments of the international club game. The Italian-Dutch domination of what was now formally entitled the UEFA Champions League – no longer the European Champion Clubs Cup – continued.

Milan's hopes of a record-equalling sixth Cup were wrecked in 1995 when they lost 1–0 to a revived Ajax in Vienna – Patrick Kluivert, ultimately to join Milan in the summer of 1997, scored the winner. Ajax then surrendered the Cup a year later to Italy – losing on penalties to Juventus in Rome.

"This is for real," said Juventus executive Roberto Bettega. "We have never really considered 1985 as a victory because of what happened in the Heysel stadium. We have waited a long time for this ... "

A long wait, but not a long reign. Juventus reached the Final again in both 1997 and 1998 and lost each time. First they went down 3–1 in Munich to Borussia Dortmund. Then, a year later, they lost 1–0 in Amsterdam to ... Real Madrid.

Predrag Mijatovic scored the goal which handed him a place in the European history books alongside the likes of Di Stefano, Gento and Puskas, Madrid heroes from another era. His goal also proved something else – that tradition counts for so much ... even in the European Cup.

The publishers would like to thank the following sources for their kind permission to reproduce the pictures in this book:

Allsport U.K. Ltd./Jack Atley 44/Shaun Botterill 3, 16, 46, 93/Clive Brunskill 42, 62, 94/Phil Cole 31, 82-3, 96/Nuno Corriea 54/Stu Forster 84/Ross Kinnaird 86-7/Craig Prentis 85/Gary M. Prior 4, 74/Ben Radford 28, 37, 57/ Mark Thompson 20, 33, 58, 60/Claudio Villa 17, 22, 80

Associated Press 91

EMPICS/Matthew Ashton 11, 14, 19, 34, 78/Jon Buckle 9, 25/David Rawcliffe 13, 51/Paul Marriott 41/ Tony Marshall 8, 53, 71/Michael Steele 26/Leo Vogelzang 73

Hulton Getty 89, 90

Mark Leech Photography/Michael Craig 6-7

PA News 76/Derrick Ceyrac 66/EPA European Press Agency 38, 49, 64/J. L. Pino 68

Every effort has been made to acknowledge correctly and contact the source and/copyright holder of each picture, and Carlton Books Limited apologises for any unintentional errors or omissions which will be corrected in future editions of this book.